Headhunter – Hunting Safaris Around the Globe: Australia Edition

JOSHUA GODFREY

Contents

About the Author

Joshua Godfrey is an acclaimed author, seasoned adventurer, and dedicated conservationist known for his extensive expertise in hunting and fishing. With a passion deeply rooted in the great outdoors, Joshua has brought his wealth of knowledge and global experiences to the pages of "Headhunter – Hunting Safaris Around the Globe (Australia Edition)," an unparalleled guide to the diverse species inhabiting the continent. Drawing from a lifetime of exploration and a profound understanding of nature's intricacies, Joshua Godfrey has meticulously compiled a comprehensive resource that delves into the habitats, behavior, equipment requirements, hunting techniques, and conservation efforts surrounding Australia.

His commitment to portraying a holistic view of hunting, one that intertwines skill with conservation, shines through in every chapter of this exceptional book. Joshua's journey into the realm of hunting and outdoor pursuits began long before his career as an author. As the founder and operator of an esteemed international hunting and fishing agency, he has traversed the globe, exploring the untamed corners of all six main continents, along with captivating destinations like New Zealand and the United Kingdom. His firsthand experiences have allowed him to immerse himself in diverse cultures and landscapes, enriching his understanding of the delicate balance between humanity and the natural world.

Joshua is also the visionary author behind the acclaimed "Headhunters: Hunting Safaris Around the Globe" series of books, which have captivated readers with their enthralling narratives of hunting expeditions spanning the planet.

Through his writing, he masterfully brings to life the excitement of the hunt, the awe of encountering majestic creatures, and the significance of responsible hunting practices.

Beyond his professional pursuits, Joshua Godfrey is a loving father to two beautiful daughters who share in his passion for exploration and adventure. Together, they embark on journeys that not only strengthen their familial bonds but also instill in them a deep appreciation for nature's wonders. Joshua's commitment to service is further exemplified by his honorable service in the US Air Force during Operation Iraqi Freedom. His dedication to protecting both his nation and the natural world underscores his multifaceted character as an author, conservationist, and advocate for responsible outdoor Experiences.

In the "Headhunter – Hunting Safaris Around the Globe (Australia Edition)," Joshua Godfrey invites readers to embark on a captivating journey through the wild landscapes of Australia, bridging the gap between the thrill of the hunt and the imperative of conservation. With his diverse array of experiences and unwavering dedication to preserving the beauty of the natural world, Joshua continues to inspire both novice and seasoned adventurers alike.

Dedication

To my beloved daughters Bianca and Zafiro Godfrey,

This book is dedicated to you both with all my heart. Your love and support have been my inspiration throughout this journey, and I am eternally grateful for your unwavering encouragement.

May this book serve as a testament to the love and devotion I have for you both, and may it inspire you to follow your dreams wherever they may lead.

With all my love, Dad

Acknowledgment

I want to acknowledge all the outstanding outfitters, professional hunters, and staff helping hunters achieve their goals every season and give them an experience they can share and enjoy for a lifetime and conservation of hunting for future generations.

Introduction

Welcome to Australian Hunting: An Overview

Most people connect to Australia with travel, surfing, crocodiles, kangaroos, and koala bears; however, this enormous nation offers a diverse range of topography and hunting possibilities. With its diverse landscapes and exciting adventure opportunities, Australia is a vast and untamed continent that draws hunters in. Welcome to the world of Australian hunting, where going after a game is more than just a sport—it's an immersive experience involving legendary cultures, difficult terrain, and close encounters with rare wildlife.

It's like entering a land of contrasts when you go hunting in Australia. The nation reveals a kaleidoscope of terrains, from the sunburned expanses of the Outback to the dense eucalyptus forests of the Great Dividing Range. Every step is an adventure into the unknown, where the scenery can suddenly turn from lush to lifeless in an instant.

The diversity of Australia's ecosystems is a playground for hunters seeking variety. Stroll through Queensland's tangled undergrowth rainforest, where the sounds of exotic birds fill the air. Alternatively, take on a challenging task by tracking elusive prey through the rust-colored sands of the Northern Territory's vast red deserts. Australia provides a constantly changing landscape for your hunting adventures, regardless of your interests.

In the heart of Australian hunting lies the exhilaration of the chase. Whether you are tracking the swift-footed kangaroo across open plains or stealthily navigating the dense bush to get a glimpse of the elusive brumby, each pursuit is a thrilling journey. The terrain demands adaptability, and the game requires a keen understanding of their behavior and habitats.

Feel the rush as you cast a line into the pristine waters, hoping for a tug that signals the presence of the mighty Murray cod or the iconic barramundi. The waterways of Australia, teeming with diverse aquatic life, offer a dynamic and challenging arena for hunters who prefer the serenity of fishing to the intensity of land pursuits.

Australian hunting is not just about the thrill of the hunt; it is a commitment to conservation. In a country known for its unique and often fragile ecosystems, hunters play a crucial role in preserving the delicate balance of nature. The responsibility of maintaining the sustainability of wildlife populations while pursuing a game is one that echoes throughout the vast landscapes.

Hunting in Australia is governed by strict regulations designed to protect both native species and the environment. As a hunter in this land of contrasts, you become an agent of the wilderness, helping to maintain the ongoing efforts to manage populations and control invasive species that threaten the delicate ecological harmony.

Welcome to the world of Australian hunting, where every step is a discovery, and every hunt is a connection to a rich tapestry of history, culture, and the raw beauty of the land. As you board on your hunting journey in Australia, you join a community of enthusiasts who share a passion for the outdoors, a respect for wildlife, and a commitment to preserving the wild spirit of this untamed continent.

In the chapters that follow, we delve deeper into the rich history of Australian hunting and explore the intricate tapestry of its wildlife. Get ready for an immersive experience that goes beyond the thrill of the chase, inviting you to become a part of the living story of Australian hunting.

The Rich History of Australian Hunting

Reading through the history of Australian hunting is like opening the pages of a living, breathing storybook. —one that unfolds with the footprints of ancient Indigenous hunters and resonates with the echoes of European settlers shaping a new frontier. The rich history of Australian hunting is not just a chronicle of chases; it is a narrative woven with threads of cultural traditions, adaptation, and the indomitable spirit of those who sought to conquer the challenges posed by the large and wild continent.

The Indigenous Legacy

Long before European settlers set foot on the shores of Australia, the land resonated with the rhythmic steps of its first hunters—the Indigenous peoples who, for tens of thousands of years, mastered the art of survival through hunting and gathering. Their connection to the land was deep, and their understanding of the diverse ecosystems was unparalleled.

Indigenous hunting in Australia was not just a means of sustenance; it was a spiritual practice deeply ingrained in daily life. The boomerang, a symbol synonymous with Indigenous Australians, served both as a hunting tool and a cultural token. The intricate knowledge of wildlife, seasonal patterns, and sustainable hunting practices passed down through generations laid the foundation for a harmonious relationship between the first Australians and their environment.

Aboriginal People fished, harvested plants, hunted wild game, and collected shellfish. They moved around a lot in search of fresh food sources. The fertility of their new land determined how frequently people relocated. A group of Aboriginal people may relocate practically daily in desert regions in order to obtain food. A band might remain in one spot for several months in regions with a greater variety of plants and animals, like the south, east, and coastal regions.

Aboriginal People had a rigid division of labor. Fishing and hunting were jobs for men. Women were responsible for gathering plants and shellfish for food. Hunting expeditions were not always successful and could last for several days. Australia's most popular hunting targets were wallabies and kangaroos. Aboriginals living along the coast hunted seals. Hunters had to be adept trackers with an in-depth understanding of animal behavior. They were skilled at mimicking the sounds made by birds and wild animals in order to draw them near enough to kill. While hunting, men never spoke to one another. They communicated silently with each other through touch and sign language. To disguise their smell, aboriginal hunters covered their bodies with dirt. They used spears to kill most animals but relied on boomerangs to kill birds.

The Arrival of European Settlers

The 18th century marked a dramatic shift in the landscape of Australian hunting with the arrival of European settlers. They brought with them not only a different way of life but also a new approach to hunting. While Indigenous Australians maintained their traditional hunting methods, Europeans introduced firearms and European game species that would significantly impact the continent's ecosystems.

Deer, rabbits, and feral pigs became a sought-after game for sport and sustenance. The hunting practices of European settlers were driven by a blend of necessity and enjoyment, shaping a unique hunting culture that embraced both the tale and tradition.

Adapting to the Australian Wilderness

Hunters had to be flexible to meet the demands of Australia's vast and varied landscapes. As settlers pushed deeper into the interior, they came across settings that were very dissimilar from the familiar European landscapes. The Wilds offered a challenging environment that called for new tactics and abilities because of its dry stretches and distinctive wildlife.

Traditional Indigenous hunting methods combined with European innovations produced a hunting style that was uniquely Australian, reflecting the resourcefulness and resiliency needed to navigate the continent's varied ecosystems.

The Evolution of Hunting Traditions

Australian hunting traditions evolved over time, shaped by the interplay of Indigenous practices, European influences, and the demands of the environment. The concept of "bush tucker"—food sourced from the wilderness—remained at the heart of hunting traditions, emphasizing a connection to the land and the bounty it offered.

The advent of conservation movements in the 20th century brought about a shift in hunting attitudes. Hunters began to recognize their role as stewards of the land, working in cycles with conservationists to manage wildlife populations and control the impact of invasive species. This evolution marked a pivotal moment in the history of Australian hunting, transforming it from a purely utilitarian practice to one grounded in principles of sustainability and ecological stewardship.

A Living Legacy

Today, the rich history of Australian hunting lives on in the practices of modern hunters who traverse the same landscapes that witnessed the footsteps of Indigenous hunters and European inventors. Australian Hunting is a story that embraces the opportunities and challenges of the present while paying tribute to the past through the continued looms of traditional customs and modern values.

As you board on your own hunting journey in Australia, remember that each step you take is a continuation of a legacy—a legacy that spans millennia and resonates with the heartbeat of a continent that has witnessed the evolution of hunting from survival to sport, from tradition to conservation. In the chapters that follow, we explore the intricate details of Australian wildlife, inviting you to become a part of the ongoing story of Australian hunting.

Understanding Australian Wildlife

Understanding Australian wildlife is not just an amendment but a crucial part of the hunter's journey—a journey that unfolds within creatures that have evolved in isolation, shaped by the challenges and opportunities of the continent.

Australian wildlife boasts an array of species found nowhere else on Earth. From the iconic kangaroo bounding across open plains to the mysterious animals foraging in the underbrush, the continent is a stage for a biodiversity spectacle. Hunters in Australia encounter not only game species but also a menagerie of creatures, each contributing to the complex web of life.

Australia is home to many elusive and exotic game species that add an extra layer of excitement to the hunting experience.

The brumby, a feral horse descended from those brought by European settlers, roams the rough landscapes, its wild spirit embodying the wild essence of the Australian bush. Tracking and chasing these majestic creatures through the challenging terrain is a quest that demands skill, patience, and a deep connection to the natural world.

Australia offers captivating waterfowl hunting for those who are attracted to the feathered land. The wetlands across the continent are swarming with migratory birds, providing hunters with a wide variety of bird species to test their skills. The striking plumage of ducks and the haunting calls of magpies create an atmospheric backdrop for an immersive hunting experience.

Australia's wetlands provide a splendid setting for waterfowl hunting, requiring hunters to use both skill and strategy to navigate through the reed-lined banks and predict the subtle movements of the ducks and waterfowl. With an awareness of the tides and the seasonal movements of their bird's prey, the hunter integrates into the aquatic wilderness.

Ethical hunting practices, including adherence to bag limits and respect for seasonal restrictions, are integral to the hunter's code. Hunters in Australia play a vital role in population control, especially when it comes to managing the impact of feral species on native flora and fauna. The responsibility of the hunter extends beyond the thrill of the chase to the stewardship of the land and its inhabitants.

Understanding Australian wildlife is not a static pursuit; it is an ongoing journey of discovery and adaptation. As you begin your journey as a hunter in Australia, each encounter with the unique cast of characters—whether on land or in water—is an opportunity to deepen your connection to the natural world.

In the chapters that follow, we delve deeper into the intricacies of Australian hunting, exploring the techniques, strategies, and stories that define the hunter's experience. Whether you are drawn to the hunt for an elusive land game or the tranquility of angling in pristine waters, your knowledge of Australian wildlife is the key to unlocking the exciting adventures that await you in the heart of the continent.

Chapter 1:
Australia's Diverse Hunting Landscape

GEOGRAPHY OF HUNTING

Australia's vast and diverse geography offers a unique and challenging landscape for hunting enthusiasts. The continent is characterized by a variety of ecosystems, ranging from arid deserts to lush rainforests, expansive grasslands, and coastal regions. This rich tapestry of environments contributes to an incredibly diverse array of wildlife, making Australia a compelling destination for hunters seeking a range of experiences.

The majority of the interior is made up of the Outback, which is a classic Australian hunting area. Its vast expanses of red earth, sparse vegetation, and rugged terrain are home to iconic species such as kangaroos, wallabies, and emus. Hunting in the Outback requires a deep understanding of survival skills and an appreciation for the resilience of both the hunter and the hunted in this harsh environment.

The coastal regions of Australia provide a stark contrast to the arid Outback. Here, hunters can explore the wetlands, estuaries, and mangroves teeming with waterfowl and other aquatic species. The proximity to the ocean introduces additional challenges and opportunities, as marine life like barramundi and mud crabs become targets for those seeking a maritime hunting experience.

The tropical rainforests of northern Australia boast their own unique set of challenges and rewards. Dense vegetation and a humid climate add an extra layer of complexity to hunting in these regions. Indigenous wildlife such as wild boars, cassowaries, and various species of deer inhabit these lush landscapes, providing a distinctive hunting experience for those who venture into the heart of the rainforest.

In the southern parts of the continent, the temperate woodlands and grasslands offer a different hunting environment. Here, kangaroos, rabbits, and a variety of bird species are common game. The cooler climate and more open terrain provide a different set of challenges, making this region suitable for a range of hunting styles and preferences.

Australia's unique wildlife, shaped by millions of years of isolation, adds a layer of intrigue to hunting pursuits. While some species, like the kangaroo, are abundant and actively managed, others, such as the elusive and endangered Tasmanian tiger, contribute to the mystique of Australian hunting. Conservation efforts and responsible hunting practices are crucial to maintaining the delicate balance of the ecosystem and preserving the integrity of the country's unique biodiversity.

Understanding the geography of hunting in Australia also involves acknowledging the traditional hunting practices of Indigenous Australians. The connection between Aboriginal communities and the land is deeply rooted in sustainable hunting methods and a profound respect for nature. Indigenous knowledge of tracking, bushcraft, and sustainable resource management has significantly influenced hunting practices in Australia and continues to shape the conversation around ethical and responsible hunting.

In conclusion, the geography of hunting in Australia is a multifaceted tapestry, offering a diverse range of landscapes, climates, and wildlife. From the arid expanses of the Outback to the tropical rainforests of the north and the coastal regions, hunters can embark on unique adventures that test their skills and deepen their connection to the land. As hunting in Australia evolves, it is essential to prioritize conservation and responsible practices to ensure the preservation of this extraordinary natural heritage.

CLIMATE AND SEASONS

Australia's diverse climate and distinct seasons provide an exciting and ever-changing backdrop for hunters, offering a variety of game species and hunting experiences throughout the year. Whether you're a seasoned hunter or an enthusiast looking to explore the unique challenges of the Australian wilderness, understanding the seasonal nuances can make your hunting adventure not only successful but also incredibly enjoyable.

Spring: The Season of Renewal

As the temperatures begin to rise and flora burst into vibrant colors, spring in Australia heralds a season of renewal and growth. It's an ideal time for hunters seeking an abundance of game. The woodlands come alive with the rhythmic sounds of galahs and cockatoos, making it a perfect season for bird hunters. Waterfowl, such as the majestic magpie goose, become prominent around wetlands and rivers, offering exciting opportunities for waterfowl enthusiasts.

Summer: The Land of Plenty

Australia's summer, spanning from December to February, is a time of plenty for hunters. In the northern regions, wild boars become more active, and their numbers increase. The warm temperatures also attract reptiles, making it a thrilling season for those interested in snake hunting. Coastal regions become bustling with marine life, with barramundi fishing and crabbing becoming popular pastimes for hunters with a taste for seafood.

Autumn: The Goldilocks Season

As the intense heat of summer begins to wane, autumn provides a Goldilocks climate – not too hot, not too cold. It's an excellent time for hunters to explore the forests and grasslands in search of deer, particularly red and fallow deer. The cooler temperatures make tracking and stalking more comfortable, enhancing the overall hunting experience. Autumn also marks the start of the rabbit hunting season, adding an element of small game excitement to the mix.

Winter: The Time for Trophy Hunts

While winter in Australia is relatively mild compared to many other parts of the world, it brings its own set of unique hunting opportunities. In the southern regions, kangaroos and wallabies are prevalent, making winter an excellent time for hunters seeking a more challenging pursuit. Additionally, this season offers ideal conditions for trophy hunts, as many species, including red deer, showcase impressive antler growth during winter.

Wet Season: The Adventure in Adversity

In the tropical north, the wet season brings heavy rainfall and flooding, creating a challenging yet adventurous environment for hunters. Water buffalo thrive in these conditions, offering a formidable target for those seeking a true outback adventure. The wet season is also the time for barramundi fishing, attracting anglers and hunters alike to the flooded plains and rivers.

Understanding the seasonal dynamics of hunting in Australia not only enhances the chances of a successful expedition but also adds an extra layer of excitement to the pursuit. From the vibrant renewal of spring to the diverse opportunities of summer, the comfortable conditions of autumn, and the unique challenges of winter and the wet season, Australia's climate and seasons create a captivating canvas for hunters worldwide.

So, gear up, explore the varied terrains, and embrace the thrill of hunting down under!

HUNTING REGULATIONS AND LICENSING

Navigating the vast and diverse landscapes of Australia for hunting demands a comprehensive understanding of the intricate web of regulations and licensing requirements that vary across its states and territories. At the federal level, the Australian government imposes uniform regulations through the Environment Protection and Biodiversity Conservation Act 1999 (EPBC Act), governing the hunting of migratory species and those listed as threatened or endangered. As hunters explore the specifics of each state, nuanced regulations come to the forefront.

In New South Wales, for instance, hunters must secure a game hunting license, adhere to the Game and Feral Animal Control Act 2002, and complete a Firearm Safety Course, while in Victoria, a Game License, compliance with the Wildlife Act 1975, and adherence to the Code of Practice for humane shooting of game birds are essential.

Queensland hunters, overseen by the Department of Environment and Science, require a Game License, must comply with the Nature Conservation Act 1992, and be aware of potential indigenous landowner restrictions.

In Western Australia, managed by the Department of Biodiversity, Conservation, and Attractions, hunters need a game license, must adhere to the Wildlife Conservation Act 1950, and may need special permits for specific species.

South Australia, regulated by the Department for Environment and Water, mandates a Game License, adherence to the National Parks and Wildlife Act 1972, and compliance with the South Australian Firearms Act 2015.

Tasmania, an island state, administers hunting regulations through the Department of Primary Industries, Parks, Water, and Environment, necessitating a Game License and compliance with the Wildlife (General) Regulations 2010.

The Northern Territory, governed by the Parks and Wildlife Conservation Act, requires a Wildlife Hunting License and adherence to the NT Code of Practice for the Humane Shooting of Wild Animals. This intricate tapestry of regulations underscores the need for hunters to stay abreast of updates, seek guidance from relevant authorities, and uphold their responsibility to ensure legal and ethical pursuits.

Embracing the privilege of hunting in this biodiverse continent goes hand in hand with contributing to broader conservation and sustainability goals, reinforcing the intricate balance between the thrill of the hunt and the imperative to preserve Australia's unique ecosystems.

Who can hunt in Australia?

To legally hunt with a firearm in Australia, you must hold a valid firearms license and, where applicable, an Australian game license.

As long as you have a valid hunting license from your home state or territory, you are free to hunt in any state if you travel there from another Australian state or territory without applying for an exemption. However, if applicable, you will have to apply for a respected state's game license for the species you want to hunt.

You must apply for an International Visitor Exemption from Firearms Services if you are traveling from abroad. They will also be able to assist with offering pertinent details regarding the importation of weapons into Australia. They will also know which species you can lawfully hunt while visiting.

You can hunt invasive species, including birds and mammals, all year round and do not require a game license. All you require is a valid firearms license. Invasive species include rabbits, hares, feral cats, feral goats, feral pigs, and Indian myna birds.

CONSERVATION AND ETHICAL HUNTING

It is crucial for hunters to comprehend the principles that underlie ethical and conservation hunting in Australia. This will guarantee that you don't break any laws. It's also a way to maximize your hunting experience and pay respect to the animals you hunt.

Conservation is at the heart of hunting practices in Australia, driven by a commitment to maintaining ecological balance and safeguarding biodiversity. Hunters actively contribute to habitat conservation, recognizing that healthy ecosystems are essential for the well-being of both game and non-game species. Many hunting organizations collaborate with environmental groups and government agencies to support initiatives such as reforestation, wetland restoration, and the protection of critical habitats.

One significant aspect of conservation in Australia is the role of hunters in managing wildlife populations. Through selective harvesting and obedience to established quotas, hunters assist in controlling the numbers of certain species, preventing overpopulation that can lead to habitat degradation and impact native flora and fauna. This population management approach is particularly crucial in regions where introduced species threaten the balance of ecosystems.

In some cases, hunting is utilized as a tool for conservation. Indigenous communities, with their deep connection to the land, have traditionally practiced sustainable hunting as part of a holistic approach to land management. Indigenous knowledge and practices contribute significantly to maintaining biodiversity and preventing the proliferation of invasive species.

What is ethical hunting?

The concept of understanding and respecting the animal being hunted and its habitat. Even though the animal is being hunted, it is essential for the hunter to follow the laws and make sure no animal is harassed during the process. This contributes to the hunter's safety and the wildlife's humane treatment. A fair game is what a hunter should be going for. This requires the hunters not to use electronic devices, radio tracking collars, or vehicles.

Ethical hunting in Australia revolves around principles that prioritize animal welfare, respect for the environment, and a commitment to responsible stewardship. The concept of ethical hunting is reflected in the actions of hunters who recognize the gravity of taking a life and approach their pursuits with a sense of solemnity and respect.

A central ethical consideration is the pursuit of a humane kill. Hunters undergo extensive training to enhance marksmanship skills, ensuring that shots are accurate and result in a swift and humane kill. The use of appropriate equipment, such as firearms with the right caliber, is emphasized to minimize suffering and ensure the ethical treatment of game animals.

Respect for wildlife is a cornerstone of ethical hunting. Hunters engage in a practice known as fair chase, which involves pursuing game in a manner that allows the animals a reasonable chance to evade capture or avoid the hunter. This principle aligns with the ethical treatment of wildlife and contributes to the overall integrity of the hunting experience.

Indigenous Australians, with their rich cultural heritage, have played a pivotal role in shaping ethical considerations in hunting. Traditional Indigenous practices are grounded in a deep understanding of the interconnectedness of all living things. This perspective underscores the ethical responsibility of humans as custodians of the land and emphasizes sustainable resource use in harmony with nature.

The collaboration between hunters and conservationists is a dynamic and evolving aspect of the conservation landscape in Australia. Many hunting organizations actively support and participate in conservation efforts, recognizing that a healthy environment is not only essential for hunting opportunities but is a shared responsibility of all who cherish the natural world.

Education and advocacy also play a significant role in the conservation and ethical hunting paradigm. Hunters engage in outreach programs to raise awareness about sustainable hunting practices, wildlife conservation, and the critical role of hunters as stewards of the land. By fostering a deeper understanding of the interconnectedness between hunting, conservation, and ethics, the hunting community contributes to a broader societal appreciation of the importance of preserving Australia's unique ecosystems.

In conclusion, conservation and ethical hunting in Australia form a symbiotic relationship, each reinforcing the other in a delicate dance of stewardship and respect. As hunters traverse the diverse landscapes of the continent, they carry with them a profound commitment to preserving the environment, embracing ethical principles, and ensuring that the legacy of hunting in Australia is one of harmony with nature and safeguarding its extraordinary biodiversity.

Chapter 2
New South Wales

This state offers an unparalleled hunting experience, from dense eucalyptus forests to sweeping outback expanses. With a rich tapestry of wildlife and a deep-rooted hunting culture, New South Wales is a destination that beckons both novice and seasoned hunters alike. In this unique Australian state, exploring the intricacies of the sport, its cultural significance, and the conservation efforts that harmonize with the pursuit of game.

Game Species in the NEW SOUTH WALES

FOXES
Vulpes vulpes

Foxes though smaller in stature compared to some game species, their wily nature and adaptability make hunting foxes a profound art. Foxes are often considered pests due to their impact on livestock and game birds, rendering their control a necessity for ecological balance. The hunt is special because it entails a unique combination of challenge and reward. The fox, with its reputation as a crafty and elusive creature, presents an exciting and often unpredictable quarry. It embodies the thrill of outsmarting a cunning adversary, a reward that is more than just a trophy; it is the satisfaction of mastering a challenging pursuit.

Foxes embody grace in a compact frame. Their weight typically ranges between 10 to 15 pounds, with a body length spanning from 18 to 30 inches. A striking characteristic is their iconic bushy tail and a coat that varies from red to grayish, often complemented with a white bib, a masterful camouflage in their native habitats. Foxes usher new life into the world through litters of 4 to 6 pups in the vernal embrace of spring. Born blind and fragile, these pups begin a journey guided by their mother's care and instinct.

Foxes demonstrate a remarkable adaptability to a multitude of environments in New South Wales. From rural farmlands to woodlands, and even the urban sprawl, they thrive with remarkable versatility. Their versatile nature makes them an omnipresent challenge.

The status of foxes as the masterminds of the twilight and night is well-earned. The keen intellect of foxes renders them an intriguing challenge for the discerning hunter. As omnivorous opportunists, foxes engage in a wide-ranging diet encompassing small mammals, birds, insects, fruits, and carrion. Their resourcefulness ensures their survival in diverse ecosystems, adding complexity to the hunt.

The lure of fox hunting extends beyond the actual hunt. It is a unique endeavor because it emphasizes moral wildlife management's value while celebrating the complex relationship between man and environment.

In the hushed hours of twilight, as day merges with night, the fox calls upon the hunter. This is the essence of fox hunting—an intricate dance that melds human strategy and the enigmatic spirit of the fox, a timeless art that harmonizes with the rhythms of nature. It's a testament to the deep connection between humanity and the wild, celebrating the allure of the hunt, and the enduring respect for these elusive creatures.

WILD TURKEY
Meleagris gallopavo

Wild turkeys, with their striking plumage and evocative calls, offer a thrilling quest for the hunters. This magnificent game bird, renowned for its grandeur and adaptability, presents a captivating challenge for hunters.

Wild turkeys, often termed "thunder chickens" for their booming gobbles, are marked by resplendent plumage and strikingly fan-shaped tails. The wild turkey boasts vibrant plumage with iridescent hues Male turkeys, or toms, exhibit an impressive array of iridescent colors, shades of copper and green that shimmer in the sunlight, while females, known as hens, exude a more subtle elegance in their earth-toned attire, aiding in their camouflage. Their appearance evokes a sense of awe in the heart of any hunter. The turkey's vocalizations are a symphony in the woods. The melodious gobble of a tom and the soft clucks of hens echo through the forest, evoking a primal thrill for hunters.

Pursuing wild turkeys requires a keen understanding of their behavior. Hunters employ strategies that range from setting up blinds and decoys to utilizing calls to lure in their quarry. The hunt often involves the use of camouflage and stealth to approach these keen-sighted birds.

The hunt hinges on the hunter's ability to adapt, read the landscape, and understand the complexities of turkey behavior. The wild turkey's extraordinary vision and wariness make each encounter an exhilarating test of skill. The rich and flavorful meat of the wild turkey serves as a gratifying reward.

Wild turkeys, with their remarkable visual acuity and keen senses, epitomize both challenge and enigma. They are active during the day, foraging for seeds, insects, and plant matter with an uncanny ability to detect danger.

Wild turkey hunting is a unique challenge that offers a blend of reward and fulfillment. These birds, with their extraordinary vision and inherent wariness, provide an exhilarating test of skill. The flavorful meat of the wild turkey is a culinary delight, and yet, it is the bond between the hunter and the natural world that truly elevates the experience.

In the heart of woodlands and meadows, the wild turkey summons the hunter to embark on a journey that blends artistry, strategy, and reverence for the wild. This is the essence of wild turkey hunting—exploring the wild's bounty.

FERAL GOATS
Capra aegagrus hircus

With its blend of challenge and grandeur, goat hunting is a captivating experience that immerses hunters in the natural world. Celebrated for their striking appearance and resilience, offer a unique and rewarding challenge.

Distinguished by their characteristic horns and sturdy physique, goats emanate an untamed and savage aura. Both male and female goats, known as bucks and does, possess horns, but the bucks' horns tend to be larger and more imposing. Their thick fur and sturdy hooves are adapted for life in the harshest terrains. Goats vary in size depending on the species. A large male goat may weigh between 200 to 300 pounds, while females are generally smaller. Goats can measure from 50 to 60 inches, including their body and tail.

Goats are highly adaptable and can be found in a diverse range of landscapes, from arid deserts to lush woodlands. In New South Wales, they roam across various terrains, seeking sustenance and shelter in rocky outcrops and bushy scrubland. Goats are known for their agility and adaptability. Their climbing prowess allows them to navigate steep cliffs and rocky slopes with ease. They are diurnal, primarily active during the day, and forage on a variety of plant matter, from grasses to shrubs.

A combination of strategy, stamina, and marksmanship are required for successful goat hunting. Spot-and-stalk tactics are frequently used by hunters, who look for herds and approach them stealthily. Given goats' acute vision, concealment and camouflage are essential. A successful hunt depends on precise shooting and knowledge of their habits.

Goat hunting is appealing for reasons other than merely pursuing a trophy. It represents a great regard for moral hunting methods as well as a deep love of the outdoors. Because goats frequently live in difficult terrain, hunting them requires both skill and perseverance. Hunting an elusive and deft target like this brings a sense of excitement and adventure to the hunt.

SMALL GAME AND UPLAND BIRDS

EUROPEAN HARE
Brown Hare
Lepus europaeus

The European hare, celebrated for its swift grace and elusive nature, stands as a distinguished quarry in the world of hunting. Its remarkable speed, combined with its adaptability, offers hunters a challenging and captivating experience.

European hares are characterized by their slender, agile bodies and long, powerful hind legs. With sleek, reddish-brown fur and large, expressive eyes, they embody the poetry of the fields. This striking appearance adds an aura of fascination to the hunt.

European hares inhabit a variety of landscapes, including farmlands, grasslands, and open woodlands. Their adaptability to diverse ecosystems showcases their resilience. They are primarily crepuscular, most active during dawn and dusk, adding an extra layer of challenge for hunters.

European hare hunting combines observation, strategy, and marksmanship. European hare hunting is special because it celebrates the art of the chase. It is a game of strategy and stealth, where the hunter must adapt to the hare's evasive maneuvers. The thrill lies in outsmarting this swift and agile quarry. European hare hunting embodies the beauty of the natural world, where the pursuit is not just about the trophy but the art of the chase itself.

In the open fields and woodlands, the European hare invites the hunter to engage in a dance that melds strategy, patience, and the appreciation of the wild. This is the essence of European hare hunting—a harmonious interplay between man and nature, where each stalk, each chase, and each encounter is a chapter in the timeless story of the hunt.

COTTON TAIL RABBIT
Bush rabbit
Sylvilagus floridanus.

The cotton-tail rabbit, with its swift movement and sneaky personality, becomes a hunter's favorite prey. Because of its exceptional speed and ability to adapt to different habitats, it presents hunters with an exciting and captivating challenge.

Cotton-tail rabbits are distinguished by their modest yet charming appearance. They possess a small, fluffy frame clad in shades of brown or gray and their trademark white, cottony tail. Their unassuming exterior adds an air of intrigue to the hunt. These adaptable creatures thrive in a variety of environments, including fields, meadows, and forest edges. They are most active during the dawn and dusk, exhibiting crepuscular behavior, which requires hunters to be attuned to the shifting rhythms of nature.

The accessibility and pure joy of pursuing cotton-tail rabbits are what make the sport so magical. It is an ode to the limitless energy and adaptability of the wild, where the thrill of the chase itself is just as important as the trophy.

COMMON PHEASANT
Phasianus colchicus

The Common Pheasant, often referred to simply as "pheasant", stands as a cherished gem of the hunting world. With its magnificent plumage and spirited flights, it offers hunters an engaging and thrilling contest. The attraction of pheasant hunting transcends the pursuit of a trophy; it encapsulates a harmonious blend of skill and a deep connection with the untamed outdoors.

Pheasants are resplendent in their appearance, characterized by colorful plumage, long tail feathers, and striking markings. Their vibrant colors and iridescent sheen add a touch of grandeur to the hunt, making them a sought-after quarry.

Pheasants are creatures of diverse landscapes, from agricultural fields to grasslands. They are known for their daily habits, with early morning and late afternoon being their most active times. Their unique behaviors and distinctive cackles offer hunters an unmistakable challenge.

Pheasant hunting is a symphony of elements—strategy, marksmanship, and teamwork with trained hunting dogs. The rush of flushing a pheasant from cover, the burst of wings, and the pursuit through the fields make for an exciting experience. Camouflage, precise shooting, and understanding the bird's flight patterns all play pivotal roles in this hunt. The sight of a pheasant taking flight, the sound of wings beating, and the gratifying moment of a successful shot create lasting memories for the hunter.

HARE WALLABY
Lagorchestes spp
Marnine

The hare wallaby, a creature of grace and elusiveness, has earned its place as a revered trial for hunters. Often called the "shadow dancer" by those who seek it, hunting the hare wallaby is a captivating and rewarding experience that goes beyond a simple trophy pursuit. It combines stealth, strategy, and a deep connection with the untamed landscape.

The hare wallaby possesses an elegant, compact frame, with agile limbs and a bushy tail. Its soft, ash-gray fur camouflages it seamlessly in the underbrush, making it a cryptic and enchanting quarry for hunters.

Hare wallabies are adept at navigating a variety of terrains, from dense woodlands to open grasslands. Their ill-defined nature, with heightened activity during twilight hours, adds an extra layer of intrigue for hunters. The rustle of leaves and the fleeting silhouette in the dimming light create an evocative hunting experience.

What sets hare wallaby hunting apart is the profound connection to the wild and the thrill of outsmarting an elusive quarry. It's not just about securing a trophy; it's about the mastery of the hunt itself—the art of tracking, waiting, and aligning every sense with the untamed world.

HUNTING LOCATIONS AND OUTFITTERS

Nestled in the heart of Australia, New South Wales unveils a splendid tapestry of hunting destinations that beckon outdoor enthusiasts from around the globe. These locations aren't just havens for hunters; they are a testament to the natural beauty of the Australian wilderness. Each hunting ground, managed by experienced outfitters, offers a unique and captivating experience that leaves a lasting impression on those who seek the thrill of the hunt.

Outback Adventures in the Riverina Plains –

The vast Riverina Plains stretch out as far as the eye can see, dotted with swaying grasses and serene wetlands. This remarkable region in New South Wales is renowned for its rich hunting experiences. Here, hunters can pursue waterfowl, wild boar, deer, and more. The allure of Riverina Plains lies in the juxtaposition of its serene landscapes and exhilarating hunts. The stillness of the wetlands is periodically interrupted by the thundering hooves of wild boars or the graceful landing of waterfowl. The expertise of local outfitters ensures that every hunt in the Riverina Plains is a memorable adventure.

The Majestic Alpine Valleys –

The Alpine Valleys provide hunters with a captivating setting for their activities, shaded by the Australian Alps. This area has long been a refuge for hunters looking for a difficult hunt because of its lush forests, pure rivers, and variety of game. The challenge of stalking deer or navigating dense woodlands for game birds adds to the desire of the Alpine Valleys, which extends beyond the scenic grandeur of its alpine meadows and snow-capped peaks. Outfitters with years of experience in this area provide hunters with guidance through the difficult terrain so they can enjoy the harmony between man and nature.

The Rugged Terrain of New England

New England in New South Wales showcases a dramatic landscape of forests, rocky ridges, and untamed wilderness. For hunters, this terrain is a captivating quest, where the prey includes red deer, feral goats, and the elusive sambar deer. The beauty of New England is in its raw, unspoiled charm. Hunters can traverse the uneven terrain, experiencing the thrill of the chase in an environment where nature reigns supreme. Local outfitters are skilled in navigating this rugged landscape, enhancing the experience of hunting amidst the untamed beauty of New England.

The Coastal Splendor of the South Coast

For hunters drawn to the sea, the South Coast of New South Wales offers an enticing blend of coastal beauty and thrilling hunts. Here, waterfowl hunting takes center stage as the coast's estuaries and wetlands come alive with birdlife. The splendor of the South Coast is in the association of pristine beaches, coastal cliffs, and the vibrant ecosystems of its wetlands. Hunters are treated to breathtaking sunrises, and the symphony of coastal bird calls as they await their prey. Local outfitters provide access to these stunning coastal hunting grounds, where the beauty of the sea meets the excitement of the hunt.

The Charms of the Western Plains

The Western Plains of New South Wales, with their arid landscapes and vast open spaces, offer a unique hunting experience. This region is known for game such as kangaroo, rabbit, and fox, providing an unfiltered view of Australia's outback. The rugged plains stretched to the horizon, bathed in the warm hues of the setting sun. Outfitters in this region introduce hunters to the simplicity and authenticity of outback hunting, where the beauty is found in the uninterrupted vistas and the connection to the land.

Hunting in New South Wales is more than just an activity; it's an opportunity to experience the untainted and varied environments that Australia has to offer. Hunters are given an unforgettable experience from the beauty of each hunting location, from the Riverina Plains to the South Coast, combined with the excitement of the chase. Amidst the stunning backdrop of New South Wales, outfitters in these areas ensure that every hunt is not only guidance but also a deeper understanding of the land and its wildlife.

GEAR AND EQUIPMENT

Hunting diverse game species, from majestic fallow and red deer to elusive hares and wallabies, demands a versatile arsenal of gear and equipment that caters to the unique challenges each hunt presents. A sturdy and reliable firearm, be it a bolt-action rifle or shotgun, is the linchpin of any hunter's gear. Equipped with an accurate optic, it ensures precise shots, especially vital when pursuing the larger quarry such as deer or wallabies.

Apparel is equally essential, with camouflage clothing tailored to the specific terrain and season, keeping the hunter hidden from the keen eyes of game species. Quality hunting boots provide comfort and grip for traversing various landscapes, while a sturdy backpack carries essential supplies, including extra ammunition, water, and field dressing tools.

For the smaller game, such as cotton-tail rabbits and pheasants, a shotgun is the weapon of choice. It allows for effective shots on fast-moving, close-range targets. The hunter's attire should accommodate both stealthy approaches through thickets and fields and maintain the flexibility required to shoot on the move.

The pursuit of cunning foxes demands night vision or thermal optics, ensuring accurate shots in low light conditions. Alongside the firearm, predator calls and lures can aid in attracting these elusive creatures.

Turkey and game bird hunting necessitate a well-camouflaged blind, decoys, and calls that mimic the specific vocalizations of each species. A versatile shotgun that can accommodate varying shot sizes and chokes is essential for different hunting scenarios.

For the wily sambar deer, it's crucial to employ scent-blocking clothing and scent lures. A good set of binoculars aids in scouting, while a climbing tree stand or ground blind helps in attaining an advantageous position for a shot.

Packing for goat hunting means considering rugged terrain and long treks, requiring a reliable backpack and possibly trekking poles for stability. Given the agility and cunning of the European hare, specialized equipment for coursing or trapping may be employed, including ferrets or greyhounds.

Last but not least, a keen understanding of the specific prey's behavior and habitats is an indispensable tool for any hunter. Together, this array of gear and equipment caters to the versatility of the Australian hunting landscape, ensuring that every pursuit is well-equipped and primed for success.

TECHNIQUES AND STRATEGIES

Hunting a diverse range of game species in Australia requires a versatile set of techniques and strategies that cater to the specific behaviors and habitats of each quarry. When pursuing fallow and red deer, stealth and patience are key. Stalking or waiting near their feeding and bedding areas during dawn and dusk is often productive. Employing tree stands or elevated blinds can provide a strategic vantage point for a well-placed shot. Stalking and spot-and-stalk techniques are also employed. Successful hunting requires intimate knowledge of their habitat and behavior, as well as the ability to remain patient and alert.

For the swift and elusive cotton-tail rabbit, a combination of still hunting and driving is effective. Approaching quietly through dense cover or waiting at known rabbit runs can yield successful shots. Common pheasants often require a combination of flushing and pointing dogs to locate and flush birds, followed by well-timed shots when they take to the air.

When hunting the nocturnal and crepuscular hare wallaby, night vision optics or thermal scopes are invaluable for tracking these creatures during low-light conditions. As for the European hare, it's a balance between coursing with dogs and ambushing in favored locations. Effective hunting for goats often involves spot-and-stalk tactics. Glassing for goats on open terrain and then methodically closing the distance for a clear shot is the preferred approach.

For the cunning fox, it's about outwitting their keen senses. Setting up concealed blinds, using predator calls or lures, and employing night hunting techniques are essential for success. Fox hunting embraces a spectrum of methodologies, from using calls and decoys to employing trained dogs. A cunning and agile predator, the fox demands strategies that often include spot-and-stalk techniques. The art of the hunt lies in the mastery of observation, understanding the nuances of fox behavior, and the precision in execution.

When pursuing wild turkeys, hunters rely on decoys, calls, and blinds to attract these birds within range.

The sambar deer, known for its wariness, often demands a patient and persistent approach. Understanding their routines, feeding patterns, and preferred travel corridors is crucial. Employing tree stands or ground blinds near well-used trails can lead to successful shots.

Ultimately, the combination of knowledge of the game species, familiarity with their habitats, and the skillful application of hunting techniques and strategies is what sets a successful hunt apart. Adaptation to the circumstances and a deep respect for the quarry's behaviors are fundamental to the success of any hunt.

ADVENTURE AND CULTURE

Situated in the center of Australia, New South Wales provides a wide range of exciting hunting opportunities, combining culture and adventure into a harmonious blend of outdoor activities. Hunters are immersed in landscapes that stretch as far as the eye can see, creating a playground of diverse ecosystems from the rugged terrains of New England to the coastal splendor of the South Coast. Here, the long-standing custom of hunting is entwined with reverence for the land and its fauna, a cultural bond that hunters greatly value.

The adventure of hunting in new south wales, is about more than just the pursuit of game; it's a journey where one becomes attuned to the pristine beauty of the Australian wilderness. It's the thrill of stalking the elusive, the satisfaction of a well-aimed shot, and the camaraderie that forms around campfires, where stories of the day's adventures are shared.

The culture of hunting in new south wales, is a tapestry of ethics and traditions, passed down through generations, honoring the land and wildlife. It's a profound connection to the land and a way of life that respects the natural world.

In new south wales, hunting is not a mere pastime; it's an immersive experience that weaves adventure, culture, and a deep reverence for the wild, creating an unforgettable hunting journey amidst the captivating landscapes of this Australian gem.

Chapter 3:
Victoria

Victoria, Australia, offers a hunter's paradise, where the ancient pursuit of hunting meets the diverse landscapes and unique wildlife of this southern state. From the alpine regions to the fertile plains and wetlands, Victoria's expansive and varied terrain provides an unmatched canvas for hunters seeking adventure, challenge, and a deep connection to the natural world. With exciting game species, from the elusive Sambar deer to the colorful upland game birds, Victoria has it all.

GAME SPECIES IN VICTORIA

FALLOW DEER
Dama dama
Ghost of the forest

The Fallow deer (Dama dama), often affectionately referred to as the "ghost of the forest," stands as a prized quarry in hunting. Renowned for its elegance and adaptability, the Fallow deer offers an exquisite challenge for hunters. Fallow deer are known for their distinctive physical characteristics. They exhibit sexual dimorphism, with males (bucks) generally being larger than females (does). Bucks typically weigh between 130 to 220 pounds and stand about 32 to 42 inches at the shoulder. Their most iconic feature is their palmate antlers, which develop in a wide range of shapes and sizes, adding to their allure. Fallow deer have a reddish-brown coat with white spots, a coloration that becomes a striking contrast against the greenery of their habitat. Its striking

49

appearance, characterized by palmate antlers and a spotted coat, adds an air of majesty to the hunting experience.

In New South Wales, Fallow deer thrive in various habitats, from temperate forests to grasslands. They are often found in woodlands, offering a mixture of open areas for feeding and dense cover for protection. Fallow deer typically give birth to a single fawn, although twins are not uncommon. Fawning occurs in late spring, with females seeking secluded areas for protection. The spotted fawns are precocial, gaining the ability to stand and walk shortly after birth.

Fallow deer hunting is an art that combines stealth, patience, and precision. They are known for their wariness and keen senses. They are crepuscular animals, most active during dawn and dusk, often retreating to thicker cover during the day.

Their herding behavior offers them safety in numbers, as they maintain a social structure within their groups. These elusive creatures are masters of camouflage, seamlessly blending into their woodland habitats. Tracking Fallow deer through forests and grasslands demands a profound understanding of their behavior, feeding patterns, and migration routes.

Fallow deer hunting holds a distinct allure for hunters. Their remarkable beauty, challenging behavior, and delicious venison make them a prized quarry. The palmate antlers, in particular, are coveted by hunters and collectors. The challenge of hunting Fallow deer lies in their sharp senses and ability to elude predators, adding an element of excitement and satisfaction to the pursuit. With its mild and delicate flavor, the

Fallow deer's succulent venison serves as a fitting reward for its tenacity. Beyond the hunt, Fallow deer embodies the deep connection between the hunter and the wild, fostering respect for the natural world and a sense of stewardship for these magnificent creatures.

RED DEER
Cervus elaphus
Monarch of the woods

The red deer, hailed as the "monarch of the woods" in hunting circles, epitomizes elegance and grandeur in the world of big game. Red deer hunting is an endeavor that demands not only skill but a profound connection to the wild. An iconic species, with their striking antlers and robust physique, they stand as the crowned monarchs of the European hunting tradition. Hunting the red deer is an art, a pursuit that marries finesse with adrenaline, steeped in tradition and camaraderie.

Red deer, particularly mature stags, exemplify magnificence in the animal kingdom. These majestic creatures boast an impressive stature, with males typically weighing between 300 to 500 pounds and measuring around 4 to 5 feet at the shoulder. Their iconic antlers, with their distinctive tines, can span over three feet in length. These antlers, a symbol of maturity and dominance, add to the aura of the red stag. The coat of the red deer is a rich chestnut-red, punctuated by a light rump patch and a dark mane.

Red deer are known for their keen senses, especially their acute hearing and vision. They are most active during dawn and dusk, embracing a lifestyle of raptors. Their social structure is defined by herds, led by a dominant stag during the rut (mating season). These herds provide protection and support for the species in a variety of environments.

The rut is a particularly exciting time for hunters, as stags become more vocal and territorial, responding to calls that mimic the sounds of rival stags. This period is ideal for pursuing mature trophy stags.

The red deer holds a special place in the hearts of hunters. Its grandeur, challenging behavior, and the potential for harvesting a trophy stag make it a prized quarry. Beyond the hunt, the red deer embodies tradition, skill, and a deep appreciation for the natural world.

The unpredictable nature of the hunt, combined with the uneven terrain where they are often found, adds an element of excitement and unpredictability. The satisfaction of a successful red deer hunt is unparalleled, with the opportunity to harvest a trophy animal and enjoy the delectable venison prized by gourmets worldwide.

SAMBAR DEER
Rusa unicolor

The Sambar deer, often reverently called the "phantom of the woods," celebrated for its mystery, adaptability, and imposing presence, the Sambar deer offers a captivating challenge to hunters. With its imposing size, rugged countenance, and majestic antlers, it commands both respect and fascination.

Sambar deer rank among the largest of all deer species, with mature stags achieving weights that can surpass 600 pounds. They stand between 3.5 to 4.5 feet at the shoulder. The defining feature is their distinctive antlers, which can span over 40 inches. Their appearance is characterized by a dark, shaggy coat, often adorned with a striking white rump patch.

Sambar deer display an adaptive nature and can be found in a variety of habitats within New South Wales, favoring dense woodlands, montane forests, and open grasslands. They frequently inhabit remote and rugged terrains that offer them a combination of cover and forage.

Sambar deer have earned their reputation as creatures of remarkable wariness and are often most active during the late evening and early morning hours. Similar to the fallow deer, they are adept at concealing themselves in thick cover during the day, relying on their acute senses, particularly their extraordinary hearing, to detect potential threats.

Sambar deer hunting is an endeavor that requires a strong sense of connection to nature in addition to skill. The appeal of this pursuit lies in the challenge of hunting an animal that combines immense size with an extraordinary ability to elude detection. It is the thrill of outsmarting such a cunning and impressive game animal that draws hunters to the quest.

Deep in the heart of wilderness areas and thick forests, the Sambar deer invites the hunter to take a journey that combines patience, strategy, and the utmost respect for nature. Sambar deer hunting is fundamentally a methodical and profound dance between the human race and the elusive "phantom of the woods."

RUSA DEER

In the heart of Australia's diverse landscapes, an elegant and elusive creature, Rusa unicolor, commonly known as the Rusa deer, has established its presence. This chapter embarks on an exploration of the captivating world of Rusa deer hunting, from their historical introduction to the intricacies of pursuing these magnificent creatures.

The enchanting story of Rusa deer in Australia begins with their arrival in the 19th century. Initially introduced for recreational hunting, these creatures found a new home in the varied terrains of the continent. This chapter unravels the historical tapestry, tracing the footsteps of Rusa deer as they adapted and flourished in their adopted land.

Habitat and Distribution

From the dense woodlands to open grasslands, Rusa deer have carved a niche in various habitats across Australia. This section delves into the ecological preferences of Rusa deer, providing valuable insights for hunters seeking to engage with these elusive beings.

Physical Characteristics and Antlers

Painting a vivid picture of Rusa deer, this chapter explores their physical attributes. While not the largest in size, their build, distinctive coat, and moderately sized antlers contribute to their unique charm. Understanding these characteristics becomes crucial for hunters navigating the challenges of pursuit.

The Challenge of Rusa Deer Hunting

Renowned for their wariness and agility, Rusa deer present a challenge that beckons hunters to test their skills. This section unravels the specific challenges encountered when pursuing Rusa deer, emphasizing the art of outsmarting their keen senses and navigating the rugged terrains they call home.

Preferred Hunting Methods

Hunting Rusa deer is a strategic endeavor. From stalking through dense vegetation to selecting elevated vantage points, this part of the chapter unveils the preferred hunting methods embraced by enthusiasts. Each method is a calculated dance between the hunter and the elusive Rusa deer, adding to the allure of the pursuit.

Trophy Hunting and Conservation

Beyond the thrill of the hunt, Rusa deer hunting holds cultural and recreational significance. This section explores the concept of trophy hunting, shedding light on its role in game management and wildlife conservation. Hunters become stewards of the environment, contributing to the delicate balance of ecosystems.

Cultural and Recreational Significance

The chapter expands its focus to the broader significance of Rusa deer hunting. It delves into the cultural and recreational dimensions, emphasizing the shared experiences of hunters and their profound connection with the Australian wilderness.

Ethical Considerations and Conclusion

As the journey through the mystique of Rusa deer hunting concludes, the final section reflects on the ethical considerations inherent in this pursuit. Safety, adherence to regulations, and responsible practices are highlighted, underlining the commitment to the sustainability of Rusa deer populations and the enduring legacy of this cherished activity in Australia.

SMALL GAME AND UPLAND BIRDS

MOUNTAIN DUCK
Chenonetta jubata
Highland Pursuits

The Mountain Duck (Chenonetta jubata), often heralded as the prize of highland pursuits in Australia, captivates hunters with its unique characteristics and the allure of challenging landscape. Renowned for its distinctive appearance, this species stands out among waterfowl, making it an exciting quarry for avid hunters. Mountain Ducks also exhibit sexual dimorphism, with males boasting vivid feathers, including a striking white head, while females contribute to the overall elegance of the species with more subdued colors. Their medium to large size and adaptability to varied environments, from highland lakes to lowland wetlands, add to the appeal of pursuing this species.

Hunters are drawn to the Mountain Duck not only for its challenging nature but also for its delicious and sought-after meat. The ducks are known for their adeptness at navigating diverse landscapes, making tracking and hunting a test of skill and strategy. During the breeding season, the ducks engage in intricate courtship displays, adding a dynamic element to the pursuit. The Mountain Duck's nesting habits, often in concealed locations amidst vegetation, provide an additional layer of challenge for hunters seeking their prized quarry.

The excitement of Mountain Duck hunting lies in the species' elusive behavior and keen senses. Hunters find themselves engaged in a pursuit that demands patience, stealth, and a deep understanding of the ducks' habits. Mountain Ducks, too, are most active during the early morning and late evening, requiring hunters to navigate challenging terrains under varying light conditions. Their social structure, herding behavior, and mastery of camouflage make them elusive targets, adding an element of thrill to the hunting experience.

Beyond the thrill of the chase, the Mountain Duck is valued for its succulent meat, making it a coveted species for hunters. The combination of its challenging nature, beautiful plumage, and culinary appeal establishes the Mountain Duck as a prized quarry, fostering a sense of achievement and satisfaction among those who embark on the pursuit. In the highlands of Australia, where these ducks roam, the Mountain Duck hunting tradition not only exemplifies the prowess of hunters but also underscores the delicate balance between man and the wild.

CHESTNUT TEAL
Anas Castanea
Autumnal Aviators

The Chestnut Teal (Anas castanea), often hailed as the "autumnal aviators" of Victoria, Australia, grace the wetlands with their distinctive characteristics, capturing the attention of birdwatchers and wildlife enthusiasts alike. Recognized for their compact size and striking chestnut-colored plumage, Chestnut Teals add a touch of warmth to the cool waters they inhabit. These ducks exhibit sexual dimorphism, with males displaying vibrant chestnut hues that become particularly pronounced during the breeding season. The females, while more subtly colored, contribute to the overall elegance of the species. Chestnut Teals are often found dabbling in shallow wetlands, feasting on a diet that includes aquatic plants, insects, and small crustaceans.

In Victoria, these avian residents showcase adaptability by thriving in a variety of aquatic habitats, from coastal lagoons to inland lakes. Their nesting habits are concealed among dense vegetation, where females carefully lay clutches of eggs, marking the beginning of a new generation. The ducklings, adorned with downy feathers, quickly take to the water, guided by their vigilant mothers.

Observing Chestnut Teals requires a patient and observant eye, as they are most active during the early morning and late evening. Their synchronized movements on the water and distinctive vocalizations contribute to the enchanting ambiance of Victoria's wetlands. These ducks are not only a visual delight but also play a crucial role in maintaining ecosystem health by contributing to nutrient cycling and controlling insect populations.

For waterfowl enthusiasts, the Chestnut Teal embodies the allure of autumn in Victoria, a season reflected in their rich plumage. While not pursued for hunting as intensively as other waterfowl, these ducks nonetheless represent a unique and cherished aspect of the region's avian diversity. The Chestnut Teal's presence serves as a reminder of the delicate balance between wildlife and their habitats, fostering a deeper appreciation for the natural world in Victoria's wetlands.

AUSTRALIAN WOOD DUCK
Chenonetta jubata
Woodland Wanderers

The Australian Wood Duck, also known as Chenonetta jubata, emerges as a sought-after target for hunters in the woodlands of Australia. Celebrated for its distinctive characteristics, this species adds a unique dimension to the world of waterfowl hunting. The male Wood Duck showcases a vibrant and eye-catching combination of chestnut and dark plumage, while the female contributes to the overall charm with her more subtly colored feathers. Medium to large in size, Wood Ducks navigate diverse environments, from woodland lakes to rivers, making them an exciting quarry for hunters exploring the Australian wilderness.

Hunters are drawn to the Australian Wood Duck not only for its challenging nature but also for the culinary delight it promises. These ducks are known for their resourcefulness in utilizing woodland habitats, creating an exhilarating challenge for hunters who must navigate the intricate landscapes. The nesting habits of Wood Ducks, often in tree hollows or concealed locations amidst vegetation, elevate the challenge for hunters seeking this prized game.

The allure of Australian Wood Duck hunting lies in the species' elusive behavior and the thrill of navigating woodlands during pursuit. These ducks exhibit crepuscular activity, making them most active during dawn and dusk, adding difficulty for hunters. Their herding behavior and ability to blend seamlessly into their wooded surroundings make them a challenging yet rewarding target for those seeking the thrill of the chase.

Beyond the excitement of the hunt, the Australian Wood Duck offers a culinary reward, with its meat known for its succulence and flavor. The combination of the species' challenging behavior, distinct woodland habitat, and the delectable reward of its meat establishes the Australian Wood Duck as a prized and cherished target for hunters.

HUNTING LOCATIONS AND OUTFITTERS

Victoria, Australia, reveals itself as a tapestry woven with the threads of adventure for the avid hunter. The state features diverse landscapes, including forests, alpine regions, and fertile plains, each contributing to the unique character that beckons with a call resonating with the spirit of the wild. For those in pursuit of an unforgettable hunting experience, Victoria boasts a variety of captivating locations, each with its unique character.

In the heart of the state, the alpine landscapes provide a challenging and picturesque backdrop for those seeking the thrill of stalking majestic deer. Amongst the towering gum trees and snow-capped peaks, hunters can immerse themselves in a pursuit that combines the artistry of the hunt with the breathtaking beauty of the high country. Victoria's alpine region stands as a sanctuary for those who appreciate the blend of skill and natural splendor.

Venture towards the Gippsland Lakes and a waterfowl utopia unfolds, enticing hunters with its wetland treasures. Teeming with an array of birdlife, including the vibrant Australian wood ducks and chestnut teals, these expansive wetlands create a symphony of nature for waterfowl enthusiasts. As the reeds sway in the breeze and the calls of various waterfowl echo, the Gippsland Lakes become a haven where the thrill of the chase mingles with the serenity of the surroundings.

For those captivated by the challenge of hunting in dense forests and open woodlands, the Strzelecki Ranges offer an enchanting playground. This region, blanketed in lush greenery and rugged terrain, is home to a variety of game, including the elusive Sambar deer. Navigating through the eucalypt forests and fern-covered valleys, hunters can immerse themselves in an experience that requires both stealth and strategy.

As hunters embark on these adventures, the assistance of knowledgeable outfitters becomes paramount. Seasoned guides, well-versed in the intricacies of Victoria's diverse landscapes, provide invaluable support. From navigating the dense foliage of the Strzelecki Ranges to understanding the migratory patterns of waterfowl in Gippsland, these outfitters ensure that each expedition is not just a hunt but a harmonious exploration of Victoria's wild allure—where success intertwines with ethical and environmental responsibility. Victoria, with its rich tapestry of landscapes, welcomes hunters to embrace the challenge and splendor of the hunt in a way that is uniquely Australian.

GEAR AND EQUIPMENT

When embarking on a hunting expedition in Victoria, Australia, it is crucial to be well-prepared with the right gear and equipment to ensure a safe and successful experience. Firstly, selecting the appropriate firearm is paramount, taking into consideration the type of game and the local regulations. Hunters often opt for bolt-action rifles chambered in popular calibers such as .270 Winchester or .308 Winchester. It is imperative to possess a valid firearms license and adhere to all firearm safety guidelines.

Accompanying the firearm, a sturdy and reliable hunting knife proves indispensable for field dressing and processing games. Additionally, a pair of binoculars aids in scouting and identifying potential targets from a distance. Given Victoria's diverse terrain, suitable clothing is essential. Opt for camouflaged or earth-toned attire to blend seamlessly with the surroundings, and equip yourself with waterproof gear to combat unpredictable weather.

A comfortable and durable backpack is essential for carrying essentials such as water, snacks, first aid supplies, and additional layers of clothing. Navigation tools like a GPS device or topographic map can be invaluable in unfamiliar terrains, preventing hunters from getting lost. As Victoria is home to various wildlife, including venomous snakes, a reliable pair of snake-proof boots is a wise investment for personal safety.

Furthermore, hunters should be equipped with a quality headlamp or flashlight, especially if venturing into the wilderness during dawn or dusk. This aids in tracking, setting up camp, and ensuring visibility in low-light conditions. Lastly, strict adherence to ethical hunting practices is imperative, and this includes using scent control products to minimize human odor and avoid detection by sensitive wildlife.

In conclusion, a well-prepared hunter in Victoria considers a holistic approach to gear and equipment. By carefully selecting firearms, knives, clothing, navigation tools, and safety equipment, hunters can enhance their chances of a successful and enjoyable hunting experience while respecting local regulations and ethical principles.

TECHNIQUES AND STRATEGIES

Effective hunting in Victoria, Australia, demands a thoughtful combination of techniques and strategies, considering the diverse landscapes and wildlife behaviors.

Firstly, understanding the specific habits and habitats of the target game is essential. For instance, stalking techniques may be more effective for elusive species like sambar deer, requiring patience and a keen eye for movement. On the other hand, sitting in a strategically placed blind or stand might be more suitable for games that frequent open areas.

Timing plays a crucial role in successful hunting endeavors. Many Australian waterfowls, including mountain ducks and chestnut teal, are more active during dawn and dusk. Thus, planning hunts during these periods increases the likelihood of encountering a game. Additionally, mastering the art of tracking is invaluable in Victoria's varied terrains. Being able to interpret signs such as tracks, scat, and disturbances in the vegetation can lead hunters to hotspots and increase the chances of a successful hunt.

Effective calling is another technique that can be employed, especially for species like ducks. Familiarizing oneself with the natural vocalizations of the target game and using appropriate calls can attract them within range. However, exercising restraint and avoiding overcalling is crucial, as this can alert wildlife to the hunter's presence.

Collaboration with experienced local hunters or guides can provide valuable insights into regional hunting nuances and proven strategies. These experts can share knowledge about specific areas, animal behaviors, and the most effective tactics for a successful hunt in Victoria.

Lastly, hunters should prioritize safety and adhere to ethical practices. This includes positively identifying the target before taking a shot, understanding local regulations, and respecting the environment. By combining these techniques and strategies, hunters can optimize their chances of a successful and responsible hunting experience in Victoria, Australia.

ADVENTURE AND CULTURE

Hunting in Victoria, Australia, is not merely an outdoor activity; it's an immersive adventure deeply entwined with the region's rich culture and varied landscapes. The state's vast expanses encompass a variety of environments, from dense forests to open plains, providing a unique and challenging backdrop for hunters. The adventure begins with the exploration of these terrains, each offering a distinct experience and requiring a specific set of skills.

Victoria boasts a unique hunting culture deeply rooted in a respect for nature and sustainable practices. The hunting community in the region is known for its camaraderie and a shared passion for both the sport and conservation. Hunters often collaborate to share insights into effective strategies, favorite hunting spots, and the nuances of tracking local game.

The culture of hunting in Victoria is also shaped by a profound connection to the land and its wildlife. Indigenous Australian cultures have a rich history of hunting for sustenance and cultural practices, and their influence is evident in the respect for nature embedded in modern hunting practices. Many hunters in Victoria value the opportunity to connect with these traditions, further enriching their experience.

Beyond the thrill of the chase, the hunting culture in Victoria involves a celebration of local cuisine and traditions. Game harvested in the region, such as fallow deer and kangaroo, often finds its way to the table, contributing to a farm-to-table ethos. Many hunters take pride in responsible and ethical hunting, ensuring that the ecosystem remains balanced and that their impact on local wildlife is sustainable.

Victoria's hunting culture also extends to the broader outdoor community, with events, competitions, and festivals dedicated to hunting and outdoor pursuits. These gatherings provide a platform for hunters to share stories, exchange knowledge, and foster a sense of community.

In essence, hunting in Victoria, Australia is not just about pursuing a game; it's an adventure deeply ingrained in the region's cultural fabric. It offers a unique blend of natural exploration, camaraderie, and a connection to age-old traditions, making it a multifaceted and enriching experience for those who partake in the pursuit.

Chapter 4:
Queensland

Queensland is a place where the spirit of the hunt meets the heart of the wild, where hunters can immerse themselves in the pursuit of a range of game species that have adapted to this challenging environment. The sun-soaked state of Australia, with its mesmerizing landscape, makes it an exciting yet difficult experience for our hunters.

GAME SPECIES IN QUEENLAND

WILD BOAR
Sus scrofa
Thunderous Roamers of the Queensland Bush

Enter the world of wild boar hunting in the wild landscapes of Queensland, where the Sus scrofa, better known as the wild boar, reigns as the thunderous roamers of the bush. These elusive creatures, often dubbed the "marauders of the outback," provide an exhilarating challenge for hunters seeking both adventure and excitement in their pursuits. Boars, boasting a robust physique, are a formidable adversary in the wilds of Queensland. With a set of razor-sharp tusks and a muscular build, these creatures can weigh anywhere from 100 to a whopping 300 pounds, showcasing their impressive strength.

The wild boar's coat is a mosaic of earthy tones, from dark browns to muddy grays, designed as nature's own camouflage among the dense greenery. Their tusks, curved and menacing, add a touch of primal awe to the wild boar's already formidable presence. Known for their cunning intelligence, these bush-dwellers are both solitary and social, forming tight-knit groups that traverse the Queensland bush with a sense of purpose.

Boar hunting, a spirited art, demands a blend of strategy, agility, and a good dose of adrenaline. These creatures are not just cunning; they possess an uncanny ability to detect the slightest scent or sound. The thrill of tracking wild boar through the thicket, deciphering their territorial markings, and anticipating their movements creates a pulse-quickening experience for hunters. The pursuit often unfolds in the early hours of the morning or as the sun dips below the horizon, adding an element of mystery to the chase.

Queensland's wild boars are not merely a trophy for hunters; they embody the epitome of adventurous conquest. The challenge lies not only in outsmarting these intelligent creatures but also in the communal aspect of the pursuit. Hunters often share tales of their encounters, relishing in the adrenaline-fueled escapades and the camaraderie forged in the heart of the untamed Queensland bush. The reward is not just in the trophy tusks or succulent boar meat but in the unforgettable stories etched in the annals of boar hunting lore. As hunters immerse themselves in the wilds of Queensland, the thunderous roars of the wild boar become a symphony of adventure and the thrill of the chase.

KANGAROOS
Macropus spp.
Queensland's Bounding Game

Step into the extraordinary world of kangaroo hunting in the expansive landscapes of Queensland, where the Macropus, colloquially known as kangaroos, transforms the hunting experience into an exhilarating pursuit of quickness and skill. Revered as Queensland's bounding game, kangaroos present a distinctive and thrilling challenge, captivating the hearts of hunters eager for adventure with a touch of the extraordinary. Kangaroos, renowned for their unparalleled mobility, boast a strong physique and distinctive hind limbs built for explosive leaps that can cover up to an astonishing 25 feet in a single bound.

In the warm hues of the Queensland outback, kangaroos showcase a diverse array of fur colors, ranging from sandy browns to grizzled greys, perfectly blending with the dry environment. Their long tails serve as a counterbalance, enabling them to execute gravity-defying leaps with unparalleled grace. The challenge for hunters lies not only in the pursuit of these agile creatures but also in understanding their social dynamics, as kangaroos often roam in tight-knit groups called mobs.

What sets kangaroo hunting apart is not just the physical prowess of the game but the distinctive thrill it brings to hunters. The pursuit typically unfolds during the golden hours of early morning or late afternoon when kangaroos are most active, creating a surreal ambiance as the sun paints the vast landscape with warm hues. Hunters eagerly anticipate these moments, relishing the opportunity to match wits with Queensland's bounding game in an environment where adaptability and quick thinking are essential.

Kangaroo hunting demands a unique combination of sharpshooting precision and strategic planning. The game's evasive tricks and bounding styles vary among individuals, adding an extra layer of challenge and excitement for hunters. The thrill extends beyond the chase, as kangaroo hunting in Queensland fosters a deep connection with the land and its unique inhabitants. Hunters become stewards of the environment, appreciating the delicate balance between predator and prey in the vast and captivating wilderness.

Queensland's kangaroo hunting community treasures the pursuit for more than just the challenge. Kangaroo meat, celebrated for its lean and tender qualities, serves as a sought-after reward, adding a culinary dimension to the adventure. Beyond the thrill of the chase, hunters forge a connection with the land, their fellow hunters, and the extraordinary wildlife that calls Queensland home. The allure of kangaroo hunting lies not just in the pursuit of a trophy but in the joy of the chase, the camaraderie shared with fellow hunters, and the satisfaction of embracing the extraordinary in the heart of Queensland's vast and captivating wilderness.

CHITAL DEER
Axis Deer
Queensland's Enigmatic Spectacle

Embark on an enchanting hunting expedition in the diverse landscapes of Queensland, where the Axis axis, affectionately known as Chital deer, takes center stage as an enigmatic spectacle. Revered for their elegance and adaptability, Chital deer offer a captivating challenge for hunters seeking an exhilarating pursuit in the heart of Australia's wilderness. Often referred to as the "dancers of the forest," Chital deer exhibit a mesmerizing grace that transforms the hunting experience into a thrilling and visually stunning endeavor.

Chital deer, with their striking physical characteristics, stand as a testament to nature's artistry. These creatures, displaying sexual dimorphism, showcase males (stags) that are generally larger than females (hinds). Stags, with their regal presence, typically weigh between 150 to 200 pounds and stand about 32 to 36 inches at the shoulder. The crowning glory of the Chital deer is their majestic antlers, adorned with a series of tines that add an extraordinary appeal to the hunting challenge. These antlers, which can span up to 30 inches, contribute to the visual spectacle of the Chital deer in the Queensland wilderness.

Chital deer flaunt a coat that varies from a rich chestnut to a vibrant reddish-brown, punctuated by a scattering of white spots that create a breathtaking contrast against the verdant backdrop. Their distinctive appearance, characterized by elegant antlers and a beautifully spotted coat, elevates the hunting experience to a visual feast. As Chital deer gracefully navigate the woodlands and open fields of Queensland, hunters find themselves immersed in a pursuit that blends excitement and aesthetic appreciation.

In the diverse habitats of Queensland, Chital deer thrive in ecosystems ranging from dense forests to open grasslands. They exhibit a penchant for both solitude and social interaction, with hinds forming close-knit groups and stags engaging in majestic displays during the rutting season. The challenge of Chital deer hunting lies not only in understanding their behavior and migration patterns but also in appreciating the dynamic and social nature of these captivating creatures.

Chital deer hunting, much like an artistic performance in nature's grand theater, demands a harmonious blend of patience, precision, and an appreciation for the captivating display of these elegant creatures. The pursuit of Chital deer in Queensland becomes an immersive experience, where hunters engage with the pulse of the wilderness, anticipating the moment when the enigmatic dancers reveal themselves in all their splendor. Beyond the thrill of the chase, the Chital deer embodies the magic of the Queensland outdoors—a captivating symphony of nature's artistry and the hunter's pursuit of an extraordinary adventure.

FERAL PIGS
Sus scrofa
Queensland's Wild Tornado

Embark on a wild and unpredictable adventure in the heart of Queensland as hunters set their sights on Sus scrofa, the notorious feral pig. Known as the "wild tornado" of the bush, feral pigs present a thrilling challenge, blending chaos with cunning in the untamed landscapes. As one of Queensland's most formidable game, feral pigs embody the raw and unpredictable essence of the wilderness, drawing hunters into a pursuit that demands strategy, resilience, and a touch of daring.

A powerful foe in the Queensland bush, feral pigs have a muscular build and a tusked manner. These animals, which can weigh anywhere from 100 to 300 pounds, move freely across the terrain. Their mottled grays to dark browns are the colors of their coarse, bristly coats, which act as a natural camouflage to hide their movements in the thick foliage. Feral pigs, with their curved tusks and unmistakable toughness, are the perfect representation of the wild spirit of the Queensland bush.

The pursuit of feral pigs unfolds as a dynamic and unpredictable dance. These creatures, known for their intelligence and adaptability, navigate the bush with a keen sense of their surroundings. Feral pigs are crepuscular, making their presence known during the dawn and dusk hours, adding an air of mystery to the hunt. Their social structure, often consisting of sounders led by dominant sows, introduces an element of strategy as hunters navigate the challenges of tracking and approaching these elusive and unpredictable targets.

Feral pig hunting in Queensland is a test of both skill and instinct. Hunters engage in a strategic game of pursuit, deciphering tracks, wallows, and other signs left by these wild tornadoes. The pursuit often unfolds in a flurry of activity, mirroring the unpredictable nature of feral pig behavior. Hunters must be ready for the unexpected, adapting to the twists and turns of the chase as they navigate the rugged terrain of the Queensland bush.

The allure of feral pig hunting extends beyond the thrill of the chase. As invasive species, feral pigs pose a threat to the native ecosystem, making the hunt not only an exhilarating adventure but also a vital conservation effort. The rewards are multifaceted, encompassing the satisfaction of mastering the wild and contributing to the preservation of Queensland's delicate ecological balance.

Catching feral pigs is a thread through the fabric of Queensland's hunting experiences, an investigation of the wild's wild nature. Hunters are forced to embrace the unpredictable by the wild tornado of the bush, which cultivates a close bond with the primordial essence of the Queensland wilderness. Hunters carry with them the unforgettable memories of a chase that perfectly captures the wild spirit of Queensland's feral pigs—a real testament to the thrill and unpredictable nature of the wild—as the sounds of the chase vibrate through the atmosphere.

SMALL GAME AND UPLAND BIRDS

GALAH
Eolophus roseicapilla
Queensland's Pink Aviator

In the expansive skies and open landscapes of Queensland, the Galah (Eolophus roseicapilla) emerges as a charming and vibrant figure, turning the pursuit of small game into an aerial spectacle. Celebrated for its distinctive pink plumage and sociable nature, the Galah offers hunters a unique challenge that combines observation, strategy, and an appreciation for the lively spirit of the Queensland bush.

With a plumage adorned in hues of soft pink and gray, the Galah stands out against the backdrop of the Australian sky. Its charismatic appearance, coupled with a colorful crest atop its head, transforms this parrot into a living canvas in flight. The Galah's sociable tendencies, often seen in noisy flocks, add a layer of camaraderie to the hunting experience.

Galah traverse a variety of landscapes in Queensland, from open woodlands to arid regions. Their adaptability to different environments showcases their resilience and introduces an element of unpredictability for hunters. The pursuit unfolds as a strategic observation of their flight patterns and social dynamics, requiring hunters to engage with the vibrant avian community.

Hunting Galah is an art that blends marksmanship with an understanding of avian behavior. The challenge lies in observing the flock's aerial ballet and selecting the target with precision. The Galah's agile flight and keen awareness demand a strategic approach, where each shot becomes a calculated dance in the open skies of Queensland.

The pursuit of Galah embodies the lively spirit of the Queensland bush. As hunters engage in the chase, they become part of the dynamic narrative written in the flight patterns and social interactions of these pink-hued aviators. This is the essence of Galah hunting—an immersive experience that combines the thrill of marksmanship with the vibrant energy of Queensland's avian community. Each encounter with the Galah becomes a testament to the dynamic beauty of the Australian skies and the lively spirit of the Queensland bush.

SILVER GULL
Chroicocephalus novaehollandiae
Queensland's Coastal Sentinel

Along the sun-kissed shores and coastal expanses of Queensland, the Silver Gull (Chroicocephalus novaehollandiae) takes center stage as a coastal sentinel, turning the pursuit of small game into a maritime adventure. Celebrated for its sleek silver and white plumage and aerial agility, the Silver Gull offers hunters a distinctive challenge that combines the rhythm of the tides with the artistry of avian pursuit.

Adorned in a palette of silver and white, the Silver Gull stands out against the azure skies and sandy beaches, embodying the essence of Queensland's coastal beauty. With elegant wings that catch the coastal breeze, these gulls navigate the shores with effortless grace. Their keen, intelligent eyes mirror the dynamic nature of the Queensland coast, adding an element of maritime mystery to the hunting experience.

Silver Gulls find their homes along a variety of coastal habitats, from sandy beaches to rocky shores. Their adaptability to both urban and natural environments showcases their resilience and introduces a layer of unpredictability for hunters. The pursuit unfolds as a strategic dance with the ebb and flow of the tides, requiring hunters to engage with the dynamic coastal environment.

Hunting Silver Gulls is an art that harmonizes marksmanship with an understanding of coastal bird behavior. The challenge lies in observing their flight patterns, adjusting to the coastal winds, and selecting the target with precision. The Silver Gull's aerial maneuvers demand a strategic approach, where each shot becomes a reflection of the coastal dance in the skies above Queensland.

The pursuit of Silver Gulls encapsulates the maritime spirit of the Queensland coast. As hunters engage in the chase, they become part of the dynamic narrative written in the flight patterns and coastal interactions of these silver-plumed sentinels. This is the essence of Silver Gull hunting—an immersive experience that combines the thrill of marksmanship with the coastal elegance of Queensland's avian guardians. Each encounter with the Silver Gull becomes a testament to the dynamic beauty of the Australian coastline and the maritime spirit of the Queensland hunt.

PINK-EARED DUCK
Malacorhynchus membranaceus
Queensland's Aquatic Artisan

In the tranquil wetlands and freshwater bodies of Queensland, the Pink-eared Duck (Malacorhynchus membranaceus) graces the waters as an aquatic artisan, turning the pursuit of small game into a harmonious ballet on the surface. Celebrated for its distinctive appearance with a soft pink patch behind its eye and its unique feeding habits, the Pink-eared Duck offers hunters a captivating challenge that blends the serenity of still waters with the precision of avian pursuit.

Distinguished by its muted gray-brown plumage, the Pink-eared Duck sports a delicate, yet unmistakable, rosy patch behind its ear—an elegant touch to its unassuming palette. With its flat, spatula-shaped bill, the Pink-eared Duck engages in a methodical feeding process, creating ripples on the water's surface that mirror the tranquility of the Queensland wetlands. Their quiet demeanor and gentle movements add an element of aquatic poetry to the hunting experience.

Pink-eared Ducks find their habitats in various wetlands, billabongs, and freshwater lakes across Queensland. Their adaptability to these aquatic environments showcases their resilience and introduces a layer of serenity to the pursuit. The hunt unfolds as a strategic observation of their feeding patterns and the gentle movements in the still waters, requiring hunters to engage with the tranquil beauty of Queensland's freshwater landscapes.

Hunting Pink-eared Ducks is an art that combines patience, precision, and an understanding of waterfowl behavior. The challenge lies in observing their serene movements, adjusting to the subtle currents, and selecting the target with a quiet and focused approach. The Pink-eared Duck's feeding ballet demands a strategic mindset, where each shot becomes a reflection of the aquatic dance in the Queensland wetlands.

The pursuit of Pink-eared Ducks encapsulates the serene beauty of Queensland's freshwater landscapes. As hunters engage in the chase, they become part of the tranquil narrative written in the water's surface and the aquatic interactions of these subtle and elegant waterfowl. This is the essence of Pink-eared Duck hunting—an immersive experience that combines the thrill of marksmanship with the aquatic grace of Queensland's avian artisans. Each encounter with the Pink-eared Duck becomes a testament to the tranquil beauty of Queensland's freshwater havens and the artistic spirit of the waterfowl hunt.

HUNTING LOCATIONS AND OUTFITTERS

Australia's Queensland spreads its colorful canvas as a center for adventurous hunters, a place where the excitement of the chase melds with the many settings that characterize this captivating area. Situated within the Australian continent, Queensland lures with a siren call that echoes with the spirit of exploration, guaranteeing a remarkable hunting journey.

The ochre-red earth meets the endless sky, creating a ruggedly beautiful tapestry of a landscape. With a variety of wildlife, including feral pigs and kangaroos, this wild area offers hunters an exciting hunt against the backdrop of breathtaking sunsets and the enduring appeal of the Australian bush. The Outback is more than just a place; it's a symbol of the pure, primal spirit of hunting.

Queensland's tropical rainforests, with their lush canopies and vibrant biodiversity, offer a unique hunting experience. As sunlight filters through the dense greenery, hunters can navigate the intricate maze of the jungle, tracking elusive game such as the native scrub bulls. The rainforest becomes a living, breathing entity, pulsating with the energy of the hunt and the charm of the natural wilderness.

Gold Coast, Queensland: A Hunter's Paradise Down Under

Australia's Gold Coast in Queensland unfolds as a hunter's paradise, where the thrill of the chase is complemented by the sun-drenched beaches and lush hinterlands. This coastal haven is not only a tourist hotspot but also a diverse hunting ground that caters to a variety of tastes. The hinterlands are home to red deer, a prized game species that challenges hunters with its elusive nature in the dense vegetation. Wild boar, an introduced species, adds an element of danger and excitement to the hunt, requiring a combination of skill and caution. For those drawn to the water's edge, the Gold Coast offers excellent opportunities for waterfowl hunting, with species like the Pacific black duck and the iconic magpie goose. As the sun sets over the Pacific, hunters on the Gold Coast find themselves immersed in a unique blend of coastal beauty and the primal allure of the hunt.

For those captivated by the coastal allure, the Great Barrier Reef unveils a different kind of hunting adventure. Venture into the crystal-clear waters, where the bounty of the ocean awaits. With outfitters well-versed in the ebb and flow of tides, hunters can seek prized catches like barramundi and mangrove jack, creating a connection between the thrill of the hunt and the rhythmic dance of the tides.

In this diverse hunting haven, experienced outfitters stand as indispensable companions. Knowledgeable guides, deeply attuned to the intricacies of Queensland's varied landscapes, become the architects of unforgettable hunting escapades. Whether navigating the expansive Outback or deciphering the secrets of the tropical rainforest, these outfitters transform each expedition into a symphony of skill, strategy, and respect for the environment.

Queensland, with its kaleidoscope of hunting terrains, invites enthusiasts to embrace the challenge and allure of the hunt in a way that is distinctly Australian. From the sun-drenched Outback to the mystical rainforests and the azure waters of the Great Barrier Reef, Queensland stands as a hunting paradise, where every pursuit becomes a celebration of the wild, untamed beauty that defines this extraordinary corner of Australia.

GEAR AND EQUIPMENT

When venturing into the diverse hunting landscapes of Queensland, Australia, equipping oneself with the right gear and equipment is paramount for a successful and enjoyable experience. The vastness of the Outback, the dense foliage of the rainforests, and the dynamic coastal environments demand a versatile and comprehensive set of tools.

First and foremost, a reliable and appropriately powered firearm is essential. Given the variety of game in Queensland, hunters often opt for rifles with sufficient stopping power, such as those chambered in .270 or .30-06, to accommodate the diverse sizes and behaviors of the local wildlife. Understanding the specific regulations regarding firearm usage in Queensland is crucial, as is ensuring compliance with licensing and safety protocols.

Optics play a pivotal role in enhancing accuracy and awareness during a hunt. Quality binoculars are indispensable for scouting and surveying the expansive terrains, while a durable and precise riflescope aids in making ethical shots, especially in the vast openness of the Outback. Queensland's ever-changing conditions necessitate waterproof and shockproof optics to withstand the elements.

Clothing that provides both comfort and functionality is a non-negotiable aspect of the hunter's arsenal. Lightweight and breathable garments are essential for the heat of the Outback, while durable, moisture-wicking fabrics are crucial for navigating the rainforests. Sturdy, comfortable boots with good ankle support are vital for traversing varied terrains, protecting against the rugged landscapes encountered in Queensland.

Pack wisely for a hunting expedition in Queensland by including essentials such as a first aid kit, water purification tools, and high-energy snacks. Queensland's climate can be unpredictable, so packing layers to accommodate temperature fluctuations is advisable. Additionally, a GPS device or map and compass are indispensable for navigation, especially in the vast expanses of the Outback.

For waterfowl hunting in the coastal regions, a reliable shotgun is essential, typically in 12 or 20 gauge, along with appropriate ammunition. Camouflage attire becomes crucial in these settings, aiding in blending seamlessly with the surroundings.

In conclusion, hunting in Queensland demands a thoughtful selection of gear and equipment to navigate the diverse landscapes effectively. By investing in quality firearms, optics, clothing, and accessories, hunters can elevate their experience and ensure a safe and respectful pursuit of the abundant wildlife that characterizes this extraordinary region of Australia.

TECHNIQUES AND STRATEGIES

Hunting in Queensland, Australia requires a combination of skill, knowledge, and adherence to local regulations to ensure a safe and ethical experience. First and foremost, hunters should familiarize themselves with Queensland's specific hunting regulations, including seasons, bag limits, and licensing requirements. Prioritize safety by wearing appropriate clothing, including blaze orange for visibility, and always informing someone of your hunting plans. When selecting a hunting location, be aware of private property boundaries and obtain permission from landowners before venturing onto their land. Queensland's diverse landscapes offer a variety of game, from feral pigs and deer to waterfowl, so hunters should tailor their strategies accordingly.

Understanding the local wildlife behavior is crucial; researching the habits of your target species helps in predicting movement patterns and identifying potential hunting grounds. Queensland's weather can be unpredictable, so hunters should be prepared for changing conditions by packing essential gear, including water, insect repellent, and first aid supplies. Additionally, it's advisable to check the local weather forecast before embarking on a hunting trip.

The use of ethical hunting techniques is paramount. Hunters should hone their marksmanship skills through regular practice and opt for clean, humane shots to minimize unnecessary suffering. Respect for the environment is integral; pack out all trash, follow Leave No Trace principles, and refrain from damaging vegetation or disturbing wildlife habitats. Consideration for fellow hunters is also crucial, particularly in popular hunting areas.

Queensland's expansive landscapes can be challenging to navigate, so developing tracking and navigation skills is beneficial. Utilize topographic maps, GPS devices, and compasses to navigate unfamiliar terrains. Finally, joining local hunting organizations or seeking guidance from experienced hunters can provide valuable insights and foster a sense of community. By combining knowledge of regulations, respect for wildlife and the environment, and practical hunting skills, hunters can enjoy a fulfilling and responsible experience in the diverse hunting grounds of Queensland, Australia.

ADVENTURE AND CULTURE

Embarking on a hunting adventure in Queensland, Australia, is not merely a pursuit of game; it's an immersive journey into a culture deeply intertwined with the land's rich history and diverse ecosystems. Queensland, with its vast and varied terrains, offers a unique tapestry for hunters seeking both thrilling pursuits and a profound connection to the local way of life.

The adventure begins in the heart of the Outback, where the red-earthed expanses stretch endlessly beneath the vast Australian sky. The Outback isn't just a hunting ground; it's a testament to resilience, echoing with the stories of Indigenous cultures that have thrived in this harsh yet awe-inspiring landscape for millennia. Hunting in the Outback is an opportunity to step into the footprints of ancient traditions, where respect for the land and its creatures is woven into the fabric of existence.

As the journey continues, the tropical rainforests of Queensland beckon with their lush canopies and vibrant biodiversity. Here, the hunting experience becomes a dance with the rhythm of nature, where the calls of exotic birds harmonize with the hunter's pursuit. The rainforest is not only a hunting ground but a living, breathing entity that immerses hunters in the mystique of untamed wilderness, unveiling a cultural connection to the ancient spirits believed to inhabit these sacred landscapes.

Coastal hunting along the Great Barrier Reef adds another layer to the Queensland hunting experience. The sea, becomes a metaphor for the dynamic cultural currents that have shaped this region. Exploring the coastal waters isn't just about the thrill of the hunt; it's an opportunity to engage with the maritime heritage that defines Queensland's culture — a tapestry woven with stories of seafaring traditions and the bounty of the ocean.

Queensland's hunting culture is also intricately tied to its vibrant Indigenous communities. Engaging with local guides and communities provides hunters with insights into age-old techniques, folklore, and the spiritual significance of the land. These interactions create a cultural bridge, fostering mutual respect and a deeper understanding of the symbiotic relationship between hunters and the environment.

In every step of the Queensland hunting adventure, the spirit of exploration is infused with a reverence for the land and a celebration of the cultural mosaic that defines this remarkable corner of Australia. It's an immersive experience that goes beyond the pursuit of game, inviting hunters to become part of a living, breathing narrative that unfolds in the vast landscapes of Queensland, where the thrill of the hunt converges with the echoes of history and the pulse of a vibrant, resilient culture.

Chapter 5:
Western Australia

Western Australia beckons to the enthusiastic hunter with its vast and untamed landscapes, where the call of the wild echoes across the expansive horizons. Nestled within the heart of this rugged terrain, hunting enthusiasts find themselves drawn to a unique pursuit, navigating through a diverse and challenging environment. From the arid expanses of the Outback to the dense woodlands, Western Australia offers a tableau of hunting opportunities. The untamed beauty of this region sets the stage for an unforgettable hunting experience, where the thrill of the chase intertwines with the raw, natural pull of the Australian wilderness.

Game Species in western Australia

HOG DEER
Axis porcinus
The Jovial Jester of the Bush Meet

The Hog Deer (Axis porcinus), affectionately hailed as the "Jovial Jester of the Bush," a delightful and challenging pursuit for hunters in the vast landscapes of Western Australia. Unlike its stately Fallow cousin, the Hog Deer embodies a playful spirit that infuses the hunt with excitement and fun. Weighing in at a sprightly 80 to 110 pounds, and standing at a modest 26 to 32 inches at the shoulder, these charismatic creatures defy their diminutive stature with a personality that captivates hunters.

Hog Deer boast charmingly small antlers that form elegant, lyre-shaped configurations, making them a unique and coveted trophy. Their coat, a rich chestnut-brown, is occasionally adorned with distinctive white spots, creating a whimsical appearance against the backdrop of the Australian bush. Known for their love of company, Hog Deer form close-knit groups, exhibiting a convivial social structure that adds a dynamic layer to the hunting experience.

These bush comedians thrive in a variety of habitats across Western Australia, from lush wetlands to open woodlands. Hog Deer are particularly fond of riverine environments, where their nimble frames and adept swimming skills come into play. Their playful antics, coupled with an affinity for water, make for a lively pursuit, with hunters navigating both land and water to outsmart these jovial jesters.

Hog Deer hunting is a symphony of laughter and strategy, a delightful dance between the nimble hunter and the spirited prey. Unlike their more stoic counterparts, Hog Deer are diurnal, reveling in the sunlight and offering hunters ample opportunities for engaging pursuits during the day. Their keen senses and unpredictable behavior demand adaptability and quick thinking from hunters, turning the pursuit into an exhilarating game of wits.

The joy of Hog Deer hunting extends beyond the thrill of the chase. Their venison, tender and succulent, is a delectable reward for those skilled enough to match the wit of the Jovial Jester. In the heart of Western Australia, the Hog Deer hunt becomes not just a pursuit of game but a celebration of the playful spirit that defines the wild, forging a connection between hunter and nature that is as joyous as the dance of the Hog Deer in the bush.

CAMEL HUNTING
Camelus dromedarius
Western Australia's Nomadic Pursuit

Across the vast landscapes of Western Australia as hunters set their sights on Camelus dromedarius, the majestic dromedary camel. Known as the nomadic pursuit of the outback, camel hunting presents a unique and enjoyable challenge, blending the thrill of the chase with the untamed spirit of Western Australia's dry expanses. As one of the region's iconic game species, camels embody the nomadic essence of the wilderness, drawing hunters into a pursuit that demands strategy, endurance, and a touch of camaraderie.

Camels, with their imposing stature and distinctive humped silhouette, stand as formidable figures in the arid landscapes of Western Australia. Weighing anywhere from 900 to 1,600 pounds, these creatures traverse the outback with a sense of regal poise. Their coarse, sandy-colored coats provide natural camouflage against the rugged terrain, and the single hump atop their backs becomes a defining feature of their nomadic presence. With an unmistakable aura of endurance, camels epitomize the untamed spirit of Western Australia's arid beauty.

Known for their keen senses and nomadic tendencies, camels roam the outback with a profound awareness of their surroundings. Camel hunting enthusiasts often revel in the early morning and late afternoon hours, mirroring the camels' crepuscular activity and adding an air of anticipation to the hunt. Their social structure, with mature males leading herds, introduces a layer of strategy as hunters navigate the vast expanse of Western Australia's outback.

Camel hunting in Western Australia is a testament to skill and camaraderie. Hunters engage in a strategic pursuit,

94

deciphering tracks, observing herd dynamics, and adapting to the unpredictable nature of the outback. The pursuit often becomes a collective adventure, with hunting parties sharing stories and strategizing to ensure a successful and enjoyable experience. As hunters traverse the arid landscape, they become immersed in the nomadic spirit of the hunt, forging connections with both the land and their fellow enthusiasts.

As an introduced species, camels contribute to the unique ecological balance of Western Australia's outback, making the hunt not only an adventure but also a vital conservation effort. The rewards are multifaceted, encompassing the satisfaction of mastering the nomadic challenges and contributing to the preservation of the region's delicate ecosystems.

In Western Australia's hunting experiences, pursuing camels becomes a nomadic exploration of the untamed spirit. The nomadic pursuit challenges hunters to embrace the vastness of the outback, fostering a deep connection with the primal essence of Western Australia's arid wilderness. As the echoes of the chase linger in the air, hunters carry with them the indelible memories of a pursuit that encapsulates the nomadic spirit of Western Australia's camels—a true testament to the exhilaration and camaraderie found in the heart of the arid expanse.

WILD GOAT
Capra aegagrus hircus
The Jesters of the Outback

Meet the Wild Goat (Capra aegagrus hircus), the mischievous jesters of Western Australia's vast landscapes, where the thrill of the hunt takes on a whole new level of excitement. Fondly dubbed as the "clowns of the bush," these goats add a dash of whimsy to the hunting scene. Unlike their domestic counterparts, Wild Goats are renowned for their spirited antics and elusive nature, turning the pursuit into a captivating adventure.

A Wild Goat, with a coat ranging from sandy brown to deep chestnut, adorned with a set of magnificent horns that spiral into an enchanting display of twisted elegance. Both males and females boast these impressive headpieces, challenging hunters to decipher the unique patterns and twists that make each set a collector's dream. Weighing between 60 to 200 pounds, these creatures navigate the rugged terrain with an agility that puts seasoned hunters to the test.

Wild Goats are the undisputed acrobats of the outback, leaping and bounding across rocky landscapes with a grace that belies their size. Their energetic behavior and playful interactions within herds make them a lively target for those seeking a dynamic and entertaining hunting experience. As crepuscular beings, Wild Goats thrive in the cooler hours of dawn and dusk, transforming the hunt into a thrilling spectacle under the Australian sunsets.

Hunters, armed with a combination of stealth, wit, and a hearty dose of humor, navigate the diverse habitats of Western Australia, from arid deserts to scrubby woodlands, in pursuit of the Wild Goat's captivating allure. Tracking these charismatic creatures requires a keen understanding of their unpredictable movements, making every hunt a test of skill and adaptability.

The Wild Goat hunt is more than a mere pursuit of a trophy; it's a rollicking adventure filled with laughter and camaraderie. The challenge lies not only in outsmarting the Wild Goat's playful antics but also in savoring the rich and flavorful venison that rewards the victorious hunter. Beyond the thrill of the chase, Wild Goats embody the joyous spirit of the Australian wilderness, forging a connection between hunters and the untamed beauty of the outback. So, gear up, embrace the wild, and let the hunt for the jester of the bush begin!

WILD DOG (DINGO)
Canis lupus dingo
The Enigmatic Nomad of the Outback

Enter the Wild Dog, or as it is more commonly known, the Dingo (Canis lupus dingo), the enigmatic nomad of the Australian Outback. A symbol of the untamed wilderness, the Dingo brings a mystique and unpredictability to the realm of hunting that keeps adventurers on the edge of their seats. Weighing between 44 to 66 pounds and standing at 20 to 24 inches at the shoulder, Dingoes are sleek, agile predators that epitomize the essence of the Outback.

The Dingo's fur, a mosaic of colors ranging from sandy yellows to deep reds, serves as the perfect camouflage in the arid landscapes of Western Australia. Their sharp, alert eyes and pointed ears reveal a keen intelligence, and their bushy tails hold a story of agility and balance. Dingoes often travel alone or in small packs, their nomadic lifestyle and elusive behavior adding a layer of mystery to the hunt.

These wild wanderers roam across diverse habitats, from deserts to forests, embodying the adaptability that has allowed them to thrive in the harsh Australian environment. Dingoes have a notorious reputation for their vocalizations, their haunting howls echoing through the night, creating an eerie symphony in the vastness of the Outback. Their cunning nature and the ability to cover large distances in search of prey make Dingoes a challenging and exhilarating quarry for hunters.

Dingo hunting is a pursuit that demands a profound understanding of the Outback's rhythms and the primal instincts of this captivating predator. Dingoes are crepuscular and nocturnal, heightening the sense of adventure as hunters track their elusive movements during the dawn and dusk hours.

The hunt requires not only skill but also a deep respect for the wild, as Dingoes embody the spirit of a land where survival is a dance with nature.

Beyond the thrill of the chase, the Dingo offers hunters a connection to the primal heartbeat of the Australian Outback. While the pursuit may be challenging, the reward lies in the mastery of the hunt and the respect earned for this nomadic creature. The Dingo, the enigmatic nomad, invites hunters to explore the vastness of the Outback, forging a connection with a wild spirit that refuses to be tamed.

SMALL GAME AND UPLAND BIRDS

SWAMP WALLABY
Wallabia bicolor
Western Australia's Enigmatic Acrobat

In the heart of Western Australia's diverse landscapes, the Swamp Wallaby (Wallabia bicolor) emerges as an enigmatic acrobat, inviting hunters into a realm of distinctive and captivating pursuit. Celebrated for its agility and charming demeanor, the Swamp Wallaby offers a unique challenge that intertwines the beauty of the chase with the allure of the wild. With a compact yet sturdy build, Swamp Wallabies showcase a warm, russet-brown fur that perfectly complements their coastal and woodland habitats. Their expressive, dark eyes peer through the thickets, adding an element of mystery to the Western Australian hunting experience. These acrobats of the bush possess powerful hind legs, enabling them to navigate diverse landscapes with remarkable grace. Swamp Wallabies carve their presence across a variety of habitats in Western Australia, from coastal areas to woodlands. Their adaptability to these ecosystems speaks to their resilience and adds an extra layer of intrigue for hunters. Primarily crepuscular, Swamp Wallabies are most active during the dawn and dusk hours, requiring hunters to engage in a strategic pursuit that mirrors the dance of light and shadow in the Western Australian wilderness.

The hunt of Swamp Wallaby is an art that fuses observation, strategy, and precision. Hunting these enigmatic creatures is distinctive, requiring hunters to anticipate and adapt to their agile movements. The thrill lies in deciphering the shades of their evasive maneuvers, adding a layer of challenge that elevates the experience beyond a mere pursuit. Swamp Wallaby hunting embodies the poetic beauty of the natural world, where each encounter becomes a symphony of strategy, patience, and the inherent elegance of the wild. In the midst of Western Australia's woodlands and coastal realms, the Swamp Wallaby beckons hunters to engage in a dance of stealth and appreciation for the untamed. This is the essence of Swamp Wallaby hunting—an immersive experience where the distinctive characteristics of this acrobatic species blend seamlessly with the artistry of the chase. Each pursuit becomes a chapter in the timeless story of the hunt, weaving together the allure of Western Australia's wilderness with the enigmatic grace of the Swamp Wallaby.

BRUSHTAIL POSSUM
Trichosurus vulpecula
Western Australia's Nocturnal Spectacle

In the nocturnal realm of Western Australia's wilderness, the Brushtail Possum (Trichosurus vulpecula) emerges as a captivating and elusive spectacle, inviting hunters into a world where adaptability and stealth become paramount. Celebrated for its distinctive appearance and nocturnal habits, the Brushtail Possum adds a layer of mystery and challenge to the art of hunting in the Western Australian bush.

Characterized by a plush, bushy tail that sets them apart, Brushtail Possums exhibit a dense fur coat ranging in color from silvery-gray to rich brown. Their large, luminous eyes reflect the moonlight, emphasizing their nocturnal nature. With a sleek yet robust physique, these arboreal creatures navigate the treetops with remarkable agility, adding an element of complexity to the pursuit.

Brushtail Possums make their homes in a variety of habitats, from eucalyptus forests to urban areas, showcasing their adaptability to diverse environments. Their nocturnal lifestyle requires hunters to engage in a strategic and patient pursuit, as these elusive creatures come to life under the cover of darkness. The challenge lies in the quiet observation and understanding of their nocturnal behaviors.

Hunting Brushtail Possums is a unique blend of observation, patience, and precision. The nocturnal nature of these creatures adds a layer of excitement to the pursuit, requiring hunters to hone their skills in tracking and stealth. The thrill unfolds in the darkness as hunters navigate the Western Australian bush, where each encounter with a Brushtail Possum becomes a test of awareness and adaptability.

The quest of Brushtail Possum embodies the mysterious beauty of the Western Australian night. As hunters engage in a delicate dance of patience and precision, they become part of the nocturnal symphony of the wild. This is the essence of Brushtail Possum hunting—an immersive experience that transcends the ordinary, where each quiet step in the darkness brings them closer to the heart of Western Australia's wilderness and the elusive beauty of the nocturnal Brushtail Possum.

RING-NECKED PHEASANT
Phasianus colchicus
The Prairie's Technicolor Phoenix

In the vast prairies and open fields of the heartland, the Ring-Necked Pheasant (Phasianus colchicus) takes center stage, transforming small game hunting into a visually stunning display of color and cunning. Revered for its vibrant plumage and elusive behavior, the Ring-Necked Pheasant presents hunters with a captivating challenge that combines sharpshooting skills with an understanding of the prairie's dynamic landscape.

With feathers ablaze in a palette of iridescent greens, blues, and rich chestnut hues, the Ring-Necked Pheasant commands attention against the backdrop of the expansive prairie. Its long, elegant tail feathers and distinctive neck ring add a touch of regality to this game bird, turning the pursuit into a visual feast for hunters. The Pheasant's solitary nature and cautious demeanor introduce an element of strategy and patience to the hunt.

Ring-Necked Pheasants gracefully traverse a variety of landscapes, from croplands to grassy meadows, showcasing their adaptability and challenging hunters to anticipate their movements. The pursuit unfolds as a strategic dance between the hunter and the elusive bird, where each step and shot are carefully calculated. The Pheasant's ability to take flight with explosive speed and navigate the prairie terrain demands precision and quick reflexes from those seeking to capture this technicolor phoenix.

Hunting Ring-Necked Pheasants is an art that requires a keen eye, steady aim, and an understanding of avian behavior. The challenge lies not only in the pursuit but also in the ability to predict the Pheasant's flight path and respond with accuracy. Each successful shot becomes a celebration of the vibrant energy and natural beauty of the prairie landscape.

The pursuit of Ring-Necked Pheasants captures the essence of the heartland, where hunters become part of the dynamic narrative written in the vivid plumage and elusive movements of these technicolor game birds. This is the art of Pheasant hunting—a thrilling experience that fuses marksmanship with the breathtaking spectacle of the prairie. In each encounter with the Ring-Necked Pheasant, hunters connect with the vibrant spirit of the heartland and revel in the challenge of pursuing a bird as captivating as the technicolor phoenix of the prairie.

HUNTING LOCATIONS AND OUTFITTERS

Western Australia, a vast and untamed canvas, unfurls its own chapter in the grand saga of hunting adventures. Here, where the sun paints the landscapes with hues of red and gold, and the ancient earth whispers tales of the wild, hunters find a playground that resonates with the spirit of the Outback.

In the heart of Western Australia, the Kimberley region stands as a testament to the untamed beauty that defines the hunt. Vast expanses of rugged terrain, adorned with breathtaking gorges and hidden waterholes, set the stage for an expedition that combines the thrill of the chase with the raw allure of the Outback. Amidst the iconic boab trees and ochre cliffs, hunters can immerse themselves in a pursuit that is as much about the landscape as it is about the game.

As the sun dips below the horizon, the Pilbara region emerges as a nocturnal realm for those seeking the excitement of night hunting. The vast expanse transforms into a starlit theater where hunters can track elusive nocturnal species such as the kangaroo and wild boar. The rhythmic sounds of the Outback come alive under the moonlit sky, creating an atmosphere where every step is a heartbeat in sync with the pulse of the wilderness.

For waterfowl enthusiasts, the wetlands of Shark Bay present a captivating tableau. A symphony of birdlife, including the elegant black swans and vibrant pink-eared ducks, unfolds against the backdrop of turquoise waters. Here, the convergence of land and sea becomes a haven for hunters, where the thrill of the hunt harmonizes with the soothing rhythm of lapping waves and the calls of coastal birds.

Navigating the vastness of Western Australia requires the expertise of seasoned outfitters who understand the nuances of this wild terrain. From the rugged gorges of the Kimberley to the expansive plains of the Pilbara, these outfitters serve as the compass guiding hunters through a journey that transcends mere pursuit. Their knowledge of the land is a key that unlocks the secrets of successful hunting in Western Australia—a land where every step is a dance with nature.

In the tapestry of Western Australia's hunting allure, each location weaves a unique story. The hunt in this vast expanse is not just a quest for game; it's a symphony of adventure where the spirit of the Outback echoes in every heartbeat. Western Australia beckons hunters to embrace the untamed, to traverse its expansive landscapes, and to discover the thrill of the hunt in a way that is authentically Australian.

GEAR AND EQUIPMENT

Setting out on a hunting expedition in Western Australia's vast and diverse landscapes necessitates careful consideration of gear to ensure a safe, productive, and enjoyable experience. Western Australia's terrain varies from dry Outback stretches to coastal wetlands, necessitating a flexible and multipurpose toolkit.

Primarily, the selection of a suitable firearm is pivotal. Western Australia hosts a diverse range of game, from kangaroos and feral pigs in the Outback to waterfowl along the coastal regions. Depending on the targeted species, hunters often opt for rifles with calibers like .243 or .308 for smaller game and larger calibers such as .300 Win Mag for bigger species. Familiarity with local regulations, adherence to firearm safety protocols, and securing the necessary licenses are imperative.

Optics play a pivotal role in traversing the diverse landscapes of Western Australia. A high-quality pair of binoculars aids in scouting expansive terrains, while a dependable riflescope enhances precision during the hunt. Given the varied conditions, opt for optics that are waterproof and shockproof to withstand the arid Outback or the coastal elements.

Apparel should strike a balance between comfort and functionality. In arid regions, lightweight and breathable clothing with adequate sun protection is essential, while resilient and waterproof attire is critical for coastal environments. Robust, comfortable boots with excellent ankle support are crucial for navigating various terrains, safeguarding against the rugged landscapes encountered in Western Australia.

Essential items such as a first aid kit, water purification tools, and high-energy provisions should be packed. Considering the often, remote locations in the state, having emergency supplies and communication devices is prudent. Furthermore, a GPS device or map and compass are indispensable for navigating the expansive Outback or dense coastal areas.

For waterfowl hunting along the coast, a dependable shotgun in 12 or 20 gauge, along with suitable ammunition, is crucial. Camouflage attire becomes pivotal in these settings, allowing hunters to seamlessly blend with the coastal environment.

In conclusion, engaging in hunting activities in Western Australia necessitates careful consideration of equipment tailored to the diverse landscapes. By investing in superior firearms, optics, clothing, and accessories, hunters can effectively navigate the distinctive challenges presented by the arid Outback and coastal wetlands, ensuring a respectful and gratifying pursuit of the diverse game that characterizes this extraordinary region of Australia.

TECHNIQUES AND STRATEGIES

Hunting in Western Australia demands a nuanced understanding of the diverse landscapes and the behaviors of its unique game species. Successful hunters employ a combination of techniques and strategies to navigate the challenges of the Australian wilderness. First and foremost, mastering the art of tracking is essential. Given the often, elusive nature of game like Fallow Deer, Hog Deer, Dingoes, and other native species, hunters must develop a keen eye for signs such as tracks, droppings, and disturbances in the vegetation. Familiarity with the animals' preferred habitats, feeding patterns, and migration routes enhances the chances of a successful pursuit.

Furthermore, the diurnal and crepuscular activities of many game species in Western Australia necessitate careful consideration of timing. Hunters should plan their excursions around the natural rhythms of the wildlife, focusing efforts during dawn and dusk when many species are most active. Additionally, understanding the significance of weather conditions is crucial. The arid climate of Western Australia can influence animal behavior, with cooler temperatures often prompting increased activity.

Patience is a virtue in the world of hunting, and this is especially true in Western Australia. Given the vast and varied terrain, hunters may spend extended periods waiting in strategic locations. Developing patience allows hunters to observe and understand the movements and habits of their quarry, increasing the likelihood of a successful and ethical shot.

Firearm proficiency and accuracy are paramount. Hunters should invest time in honing their marksmanship skills, ensuring they can take clean and humane shots when the opportunity arises. Additionally, a thorough understanding of firearm safety is imperative to mitigate risks during the pursuit.

Finally, embracing a holistic approach to the hunting experience fosters a deeper connection with the natural environment. Respecting local regulations, practicing ethical hunting methods, and acknowledging the importance of conservation contribute to the sustainability of game populations and the preservation of Western Australia's unique ecosystems. In essence, successful hunting in Western Australia involves a blend of knowledge, skill, patience, and a profound appreciation for the delicate balance between hunter and the wild.

ADVENTURE AND CULTURE

Going on a hunting expedition in Western Australia reveals a voyage that goes beyond the hunt and provides a deep bond with the expansive and varied terrain that characterizes this remarkable area. The vast Outback, where the parched plains elongate and whisper of a bygone era rich in history, is where the adventure starts. Hunting here is an experience of the untamed beauty and tenacity of a terrain that has withstood the test of time, rather than just a chase.

As hunters navigate the Outback's red-earthed expanses, they become part of a cultural narrative shaped by the rich heritage of Indigenous communities. Engaging with local guides reveals age-old hunting techniques, spiritual connections to the land, and the wisdom of survival in this challenging environment. The Outback, with its sparse vegetation and wide horizons, becomes a canvas for both the hunter's adventure and a testament to the enduring cultural traditions of Western Australia's First Nations people.

Moving towards the coastal regions, the hunting experience takes a different turn. Western Australia's vast coastline, adorned with wetlands and estuaries, invites hunters to engage with the dynamic ecosystems that characterize this part of the world. Waterfowl hunting along the coast is not just a sport; it's an opportunity to become part of the intricate balance between hunters and the abundance of birdlife that graces the wetlands. The coastal culture intertwines with the rhythm of the tides, creating a unique hunting experience where the ebb and flow of the ocean become integral to the adventure.

The cultural tapestry of Western Australia also weaves in the stories of European settlers who, over time, have contributed to the region's hunting heritage. Old-world traditions meld with the wild beauty of the Australian landscapes, creating a fusion of cultures that defines the hunting experience in Western Australia.

In every step of the journey, from the arid Outback to the coastal wetlands, the spirit of adventure is enriched by a respect for the land and its cultural history. Western Australia's hunting culture is a celebration of diversity, both in landscapes and in the people who call this region home. It's an immersive experience where the pursuit of game becomes a gateway to understanding and appreciating the unique intersection of nature, culture, and history that makes Western Australia a truly exceptional hunting destination.

Chapter 6:
South Australia

South Australia is unlike any other place to visit because of its unexplored natural riches, which range from lush bushland to arid plains. Here, enthusiasts set out on a unique adventure, overcoming obstacles in a setting that promises excitement and unpredictability in equal measure. The sound of the wild calls to this southern sanctuary, where the excitement of the chase mingles with the unfiltered, natural spirit of the Australian outback, preparing for a singularly remarkable hunting journey.

Game Species in south Australia

RED KANGAROO
Macropus rufus
Outback Giants

The Red Kangaroo (Macropus rufus), revered as the "outback giants" of South Australia, stands as a thrilling pursuit for hunters, embodying both challenge and reward. Known for their iconic characteristics, these marsupials present an exhilarating hunting experience in the diverse landscapes of the Australian outback. Boomer kangaroos can weigh between 150 to 200 pounds and stand at an impressive height of around 5.2 to 6.6 feet. Their distinctive features include powerful hind legs, adapted for efficient hopping, and robust tails that aid in balance.

Red Kangaroos thrive in a variety of habitats, from arid plains to grasslands. Their populations are often found in social groups, known as mobs, which provide safety and enhance their ability to forage for vegetation. Female kangaroos, known as flyers, give birth to a single joey after a month-long gestation period. The joey, born in a highly undeveloped state, completes its development within the safety of the mother's pouch.

Hunting Red Kangaroos demands a unique set of skills, combining patience, precision, and respect for the vastness of the outback. Kangaroos are most active during the early morning and late evening, utilizing their keen senses to navigate the terrain. Their swift movements and ability to cover large distances make them a challenging quarry, and hunters often employ tracking techniques to understand their behaviors and locate them in the wild.

The allure of Red Kangaroo hunting lies in the majestic presence of these outback giants and the unique challenges they pose to hunters. Beyond the thrill of the pursuit, the kangaroo's lean and healthy meat is a prized reward for hunters, reflecting the sustainability and balance within the ecosystem. The pursuit of Red Kangaroos embodies a deep connection between hunters and the untamed outback, fostering a respect for the resilience and adaptability of these iconic Australian creatures.

RED FOX
Vulpes vulpes
Outback Prowlers

The Red Fox (Vulpes vulpes) emerges as a spirited and cunning adversary, creating an exhilarating and sought-after pursuit for hunters. Revered as the "outback prowlers," these foxes are known for their distinctive characteristics that make hunting them a thrilling and rewarding experience. The Red Fox, exhibiting sexual dimorphism with males typically larger than females, boasts a magnificent red and orange fur coat, perfectly adapted for blending into the diverse landscapes of the outback. Weighing between 8 to 15 pounds, these agile predators possess sharp instincts and keen senses, adding to the excitement of the chase.

The appeal of fox hunting lies in the stealthy and unpredictable nature of these outback prowlers. Hunters are drawn to the challenge of outsmarting these cunning creatures, testing their skills in tracking and ambushing. Red Foxes are crepuscular, making them most active during dawn and dusk, creating an atmospheric backdrop for the pursuit. Their ability to adapt to various environments, from arid deserts to lush woodlands, provides hunters with a dynamic and ever-changing hunting ground.

Hunters love the pursuit of Red Foxes not only for the thrill of the chase but also for the positive impact on local ecosystems. Foxes are known for preying on native wildlife, and hunting them helps maintain a balance, protecting vulnerable species. The pursuit is also valued for the skills it hones in hunters, requiring a blend of patience, strategic thinking, and adaptability to the unpredictable movements of the fox.

The excitement of fox hunting is heightened by the element of surprise and the fox's elusive nature. With a reputation for being clever and crafty, Red Foxes keep hunters on their toes, making each pursuit a unique and unpredictable adventure. The challenge of outwitting these outback prowlers, combined with the thrill of being immersed in the breathtaking landscapes of South Australia, transforms fox hunting into an exciting and captivating experience.

The hunt of Red Foxes becomes more than a recreational activity; it is a dynamic and fulfilling endeavor that fosters camaraderie among hunters and showcases the beauty of the

South Australian wilderness. The distinctive qualities of the Red Fox, coupled with the strategic and invigorating nature of the hunt, make it a beloved and enduring pursuit for those seeking the ultimate adventure in the Australian outback.

EUROPEAN RABBIT
Oryctolagus cuniculus
Outback Burrowers

In the sun-kissed landscapes of South Australia, the European Rabbit (Oryctolagus cuniculus) emerges as lively and nimble prey, inviting hunters into the realm of the outback burrowers. Celebrated for their distinctive characteristics, these rabbits provide an exciting and dynamic pursuit, creating an engaging and rewarding experience for hunters. Both male and female rabbits contribute to the rabbit's charm, showcasing a soft and dense fur coat in shades of brown, grey, and white. Weighing between 2 to 4 pounds, these agile burrowers possess a keen sense of hearing and nimble movements, adding an element of unpredictability to the hunt.

The allure of rabbit hunting lies in the thrilling and strategic pursuit of these outback burrowers. Known for their prolific breeding and burrow-digging abilities, European Rabbits present a challenge for hunters seeking to control their populations. Rabbit hunting often involves strategic approaches such as stalking, ambushing, and utilizing well-trained hunting dogs, turning each pursuit into a captivating and interactive experience.

Hunters are drawn to the excitement of rabbit hunting not only for the strategic challenge it presents but also for the positive impact on the ecosystem. European Rabbits can have a significant impact on vegetation and soil structure, and hunting them aids in maintaining ecological balance. The pursuit is also favored for its accessibility and the camaraderie it fosters among hunters.

The excitement of rabbit hunting unfolds in the dynamic and diverse terrains of South Australia. Rabbits are most active during the early morning and late evening, creating an ideal backdrop for the pursuit. Their ability to dart into burrows adds an element of surprise to the chase, requiring hunters to be quick-witted and agile. The thrill of rabbit hunting lies in its versatility, offering hunters of all skill levels an engaging and entertaining experience.

In the heart of the outback, the pursuit of European Rabbits becomes a vibrant and cherished tradition. The distinctive qualities of these outback burrowers, coupled with the strategic and exhilarating nature of the hunt, make rabbit hunting an enduring and beloved pastime. The pursuit not only showcases the agility and adaptability of hunters but also underscores the interconnected relationship between humans and the lively landscapes of the South Australian outback.

SMALL GAME AND UPLAND BIRDS

WHITE-EYED DUCK
Aythya australis
Southern Elegance

The White-eyed Duck, also known as Aythya australis, stands as a distinctive and captivating waterfowl, offering hunters a unique and exclusive pursuit. Renowned for its exceptional characteristics, this duck becomes a prized target, infusing the hunt with both challenge and the allure of Southern elegance. Exhibiting sexual dimorphism, the males showcase striking white eyes, contrasting against their dark plumage, while the females contribute to the species' overall grace with their more subtly colored feathers. With an average length of 20 inches and a wingspan of 31 inches, these ducks navigate both freshwater lakes and secluded wetlands with refined poise.

Found in secluded freshwater lagoons and serene wetlands, these ducks provide hunters with a rare and picturesque hunting ground. Their diving behavior, feeding on aquatic vegetation and invertebrates, adds a layer of unpredictability and excitement to the pursuit.

Hunters are drawn to the exhilarating challenge of White-eyed Duck hunting, appreciating not only the thrill of the chase but also the aesthetic and bragging rights it brings. The ducks' synchronized movements on the water, distinctive calls, and the serene backdrop of Southern wetlands contribute to the immersive experience of waterfowl hunting. The White-eyed Duck's lean and flavorful meat becomes a cherished reward, blending the excitement of the pursuit with the satisfaction of a rare culinary outcome.

The excitement of White-eyed Duck hunting unfolds during the early morning and late evening, as these Southern elegances engage in their most active periods. Hunters often position themselves strategically in concealed blinds, using decoys to enhance the overall experience. The duck's elusive nature and exclusive habitat make each waterfowl hunting expedition a memorable and truly exciting adventure.

The hunt of White-eyed Ducks becomes a celebration of the region's exceptional waterfowl species. The distinctive qualities of these Southern elegances, coupled with the strategic and rewarding nature of the hunt, make waterfowl hunting an enduring and cherished tradition. The pursuit not only highlights the skill and camaraderie among hunters but also underscores the profound connection between humans and the pristine Southern wetland ecosystems of South Australia.

SPINY-CHEEKED HONEYEATER
Acanthagenys rufogularis
Wetland Whisperers

In the lush wetlands of South Australia, the Spiny-cheeked Honeyeater, scientifically known as Acanthagenys rufogularis, emerges as a unique and alluring waterfowl, beckoning hunters to engage in a distinctive pursuit. Renowned for its exceptional characteristics, this honeyeater becomes a prized target, infusing the hunt with both challenge and the charm of wetland whispers. Exhibiting sexual dimorphism, the males showcase vibrant spiny cheek patches, enhancing their overall appeal, while the females contribute to the species' grace with more subtly colored features. With an average length of 8 inches and a wingspan of 12 inches, these honeyeaters navigate the wetland foliage with agile grace.

Nestled among flowering shrubs and thickets, these honeyeaters offer hunters a unique and colorful hunting area. The chase is made more exciting and unpredictable by their deft maneuvers and acrobatic foraging for insects and nectar.

Hunters are captivated by the challenge of Spiny-cheeked Honeyeater hunting, appreciating not only the thrill of the chase but also the unique experience it brings. The honeyeaters' melodious calls, synchronized movements among the wetland flora, and the serene backdrop of the wetlands contribute to the immersive experience of this waterfowl hunting. The Spiny-cheeked Honeyeater's lean and subtly sweet meat becomes a cherished reward, blending the excitement of the pursuit with the satisfaction of a rare culinary outcome.

The excitement of Spiny-cheeked Honeyeater hunting unfolds during the early morning and late evening, as these wetland whisperers engage in their most active periods. Hunters often position themselves strategically amidst the wetland foliage, using their knowledge of the honeyeaters' preferred habitats to enhance the overall experience. The honeyeater's elusive nature and unique habitat make each waterfowl hunting expedition a memorable and truly exciting adventure.

Spotting Spiny-cheeked Honeyeaters turns into an ode to the area's remarkable avian inhabitants. Hunting waterfowl is a beloved and long-lasting tradition because of the unique characteristics of these wetland whisperers as well as the strategic and satisfying aspect of the hunt. It also emphasizes the strong bond between humans and South Australia's thriving wetland ecosystems. The hunt showcases the hunters' skill and camaraderie.

PURPLE-GALLINULE DUCK
Porphyrio porphyrio
Wetland Royalty

The Purple-gallinule Duck, or Porphyrio porphyrio as it is scientifically known, is the royal duck of the wetlands of South Australia. It welcomes hunters into a world of vivid colors and unique features. Renowned for its extraordinary qualities, this duck turns into a royal target, adding a sense of challenge and wetland grandeur to the hunt. The males display sexual dimorphism with their iridescent purple and blue plumage and bright red beaks, while the females add to the overall elegance of the species with their more delicately colored features. Measuring an average of fifteen inches in length and twenty-five inches in width, these ducks move gracefully through the marsh vegetation.

The lure of hunting Purple-gallinule Duck is found only in its habitat, which is South Australia's verdant wetlands. These ducks offer hunters a magnificent and aesthetically pleasing hunting area because they are found among thick reeds, water lilies, and floating vegetation. Their elusive nature, which often keeps them hidden in the marsh vegetation, makes the chase more exciting and unpredictable.

Hunters are captivated by the challenge of Purple-gallinule Duck hunting, appreciating not only the thrill of the chase but also the regal experience it brings. The ducks' distinctive calls, synchronized movements among the wetland flora, and the picturesque backdrop of the wetlands contribute to the immersive experience of this waterfowl hunting. The Purple-gallinule Duck's lean and flavorful meat becomes a cherished reward, blending the excitement of the pursuit with the satisfaction of a rare culinary outcome.

Purple-gallinule Duck hunting is most exciting in the early morning and late evening when these royals of the marsh are at their most active. Decoys and blinds are common tools used by hunters to improve their overall experience as they place themselves strategically among the wetland vegetation. Every waterfowl hunting excursion is an unforgettable and genuinely thrilling experience due to the duck's elusive nature and distinctive habitat.

A celebration of the area's remarkable waterfowl species is created when hunting Purple-gallinule Ducks in the picturesque wetlands of South Australia. Waterfowl hunting is an enduring and cherished tradition because of the unique characteristics of these wetland royals, as well as the strategic and rewarding nature of the hunt. In addition to showcasing hunting prowess and camaraderie, the chase emphasizes the close bond that exists between humans and South Australia's fascinating wetland ecosystems.

HUNTING LOCATIONS AND OUTFITTERS

South Australia emerges as a canvas painted with the hues of adventure for the impassioned hunter. The state unfolds a landscape that is as diverse as it is captivating, ranging from the arid expanses of the Outback to the lush coastal fringes, each contributing to an allure that resonates with the call of the wild. For those yearning for an extraordinary hunting odyssey, South Australia unveils a mosaic of compelling locations, each boasting its own distinctive character.

The Outback, located in the center of the state, is a well-known hunting destination. Its vast horizons and red earth offer an exciting environment for those pursuing animals like kangaroos and feral goats. Hunters can immerse themselves in an experience that perfectly combines the excitement of the hunt with the unadulterated beauty of the remote landscape beneath the expansive Outback skies. The Outback of South Australia turns into a haven for people looking for the wild spirit.

Head towards the Flinders Ranges, and a rugged paradise beckons, offering a challenging haven for hunters captivated by the allure of dense bushland and rocky outcrops. This region, adorned with ancient landscapes and steep gorges, is a prime habitat for a variety of game, including the elusive Euro and red deer. Navigating through the eucalyptus-filled valleys and rocky ridges, hunters can engage in an immersive experience that demands both skill and strategic prowess.

For waterfowl enthusiasts, the Coorong Coastal lagoons and wetlands unveil a mesmerizing tapestry of avian life. Teeming with migratory bird species such as Cape Barren geese and black swans, these coastal habitats provide a symphony of nature that enchants hunters as they navigate the waterways and hidden coves. As the calls of waterfowl echo over the tranquil waters, the Coorong Coastal region becomes a haven where the pursuit of waterfowl intertwines seamlessly with the tranquility of the surroundings.

As hunters embark on these extraordinary journeys, the guidance of seasoned outfitters becomes indispensable. These knowledgeable guides, well-versed in the intricacies of South Australia's diverse landscapes, serve as invaluable companions. From understanding the movements of kangaroo populations in the Outback to navigating the challenging terrain of the Flinders Ranges, these outfitters ensure that each expedition is not just a hunt but a harmonious exploration of South Australia's untamed allure—where success is measured not only in the thrill of the chase but in the ethical and environmental responsibility embraced along the way. South Australia, with its diverse tapestry of landscapes, invites hunters to embrace the challenge and magnificence of the hunt in a way that is uniquely Australian

GEAR AND EQUIPMENT

Hunting in the diverse landscapes of South Australia necessitates a well-thought-out selection of gear and equipment to ensure a safe and successful expedition. Choosing the right firearm is paramount, considering the varied game species, from kangaroos to feral goats. Bolt-action rifles in calibers like .243 Winchester or .270 Winchester are popular choices, offering versatility for different-sized game.

Possessing a valid firearms license and adhering to safety regulations is a prerequisite. Given the arid and expansive nature of the region, quality optics, including binoculars and a reliable rifle scope, are indispensable for spotting game at a distance. Sturdy and comfortable footwear, such as durable boots with ankle support, is essential for traversing diverse terrains ranging from rocky outcrops to sandy plains.

South Australia's fluctuating weather conditions highlight the importance of adaptable clothing. Lightweight and moisture-wicking apparel for warmer periods, complemented by layering options for cooler mornings and evenings, ensures hunters are prepared for temperature variations. Camouflaged or earth-toned clothing aids in blending with the surroundings, particularly in bushland and grassy plains. A spacious and durable backpack is vital for carrying essentials, including water, snacks, first aid supplies, and additional clothing layers. Given the vastness of the Outback, a reliable GPS device or topographic map is crucial for navigation and preventing disorientation in remote areas.

TECHNIQUES AND STRATEGIES

Successfully navigating the diverse landscapes of South Australia requires hunters to employ a range of techniques and strategies. A fundamental aspect of hunting in this region is understanding the behavior and habits of the various game species, which include kangaroos, feral goats, and an array of bird species. Stalking is a commonly employed technique, given the expansive bushland and grassy plains; hunters must exercise patience and move quietly to avoid detection by wary wildlife. Utilizing natural features like ridges and dense vegetation for cover can enhance stalking success. Additionally, the arid nature of some regions demands a keen eye for tracking, as animals leave distinct prints in the soil. Timing is crucial, with many species more active during dawn and dusk, making these periods optimal for hunting.

South Australia's vast Outback also presents opportunities for spot-and-stalk hunting, where elevated positions offer vantage points for spotting game from a distance. Strategic placement of blinds or hides near water sources can prove effective, especially during the dry season when animals congregate around limited water supplies. Effective calling techniques, such as mimicking the sounds of local bird species or utilizing predator calls, can attract certain game, adding an auditory dimension to the hunt.

Given the challenging terrain, hunters in South Australia should equip themselves with reliable navigation tools, such as GPS devices or topographic maps, to prevent getting disoriented. Collaborating with local hunters and guides can provide invaluable insights into regional nuances and proven strategies. It's essential to adhere to ethical hunting practices, including positive identification of the target, compliance with regulations, and respect for the environment. By combining these techniques and strategies, hunters can optimize their chances of a successful and responsible hunting experience in the diverse landscapes of South Australia.

ADVENTURE AND CULTURE

South Australia offers a distinctive and captivating experience for hunting enthusiasts, blending adventure with a unique cultural backdrop. The vast and varied landscapes of South Australia provide an array of hunting opportunities, from the arid Outback to coastal regions and dense bushland. The adventure begins with the exploration of these diverse terrains, where hunters encounter a range of game species, each adapted to its specific environment.

The hunting culture in South Australia is deeply influenced by the state's pioneering spirit and connection to the land. Many hunters in the region embrace the self-sufficiency and sustainability aspects of the activity, reflecting the historical importance of hunting for survival in Australia's early settler days. This cultural connection to the land is often shared within local hunting communities, fostering a sense of camaraderie and respect for the environment.

Indigenous Australian cultures, with their deep-rooted traditions of hunting and gathering, also contribute to the cultural tapestry of hunting in South Australia. The state's diverse ecosystems provide a bounty of game, including kangaroos, feral goats, and various bird species. Hunting in South Australia often involves a profound appreciation for the natural world and an understanding of the delicate balance required for sustainable hunting practices.

The adventure of hunting in South Australia extends beyond the pursuit of game to encompass the exploration of remote and untamed landscapes. From the Flinders Ranges to the Coorong, hunters have the opportunity to experience the unique flora and fauna of the region while honing their skills in tracking and bushcraft.

Cultural events and festivals related to hunting, outdoor pursuits, and conservation contribute to the vibrant hunting community in South Australia. These gatherings serve as platforms for hunters to share stories, exchange knowledge, and celebrate their shared passion for the outdoors.

In summary, the adventure and culture of hunting in South Australia are deeply intertwined with the state's diverse landscapes, historical roots, and a shared respect for the land.

It offers a multifaceted experience that goes beyond the thrill of the hunt, encompassing a connection to tradition, community, and the breathtaking natural beauty that defines South Australia.

Chapter 7:
Northern Territory

Northern territory brings out the vast expense of wildlife, it is an Australian treasure trove for those seeking a diverse and thrilling hunting experience offering an array of game species and is renowned for its significant populations of large game animals. Here, you'll find the majestic water buffalo, the elusive banteng, and the formidable wild boar, along with small games and upland birds. These remarkable species make the Northern Territory a top choice for hunters in search of challenging and awe-inspiring big game pursuits.

Game Species in the Northern Territory

WATER BUFFALO
Bubalus bubalis
Wild buffalo

Australia's Northern Territory is home to vast, untamed landscapes; a grand creature reigns supreme—the water buffalo. The water buffalo commands attention due to its enormous size and distinctive horns. They are the giants of the region, with bulls weighing more than a ton. Water buffalo's formidable horns are not only a defining feature but also a significant factor in hunting. When evaluating an animal's potential as a trophy, hunters must take the size and shape of its horns into account. Understanding the buffalo's internal anatomy is crucial for ethical hunting. Knowing the location of vital organs like the heart and lungs is essential for accurate shot placement, ensuring a swift and humane kill; they may require multiple shots to bring down.

Like most animals, a water buffalo's length can change with age, sex, and subspecies. From the top of their heads to the base of their tails, adult water buffaloes can range in size from 9 to 12 feet (2.7 to 3.7 meters). The additional length of the tail can range from 2 to 3 feet (0.6 to 0.9 meters). They prefer wetlands and swampy regions, where they can often be seen wading through mud and water, using wallowing to regulate body temperature and deter insects. They are also often found in grassy plains and savannas, as their diet is primarily composed of grasses. With wetlands, grasslands, and forests among its varied landscapes, they have adapted to these environments. Utilizing the lush plains and swamps, these hardy creatures graze mostly on local grasses. Breeding among these wild buffaloes occurs during the wet season, often leading to the birth of single calves after a gestation period of about 10 to 11 months. These buffaloes typically form small family units and are frequently seen in groups, displaying strong social bonds. Meat from water buffalo is a rare resource, lean, and regarded as a healthy and long-lasting source of protein. The distinctive flavor of buffalo meat appeals to many hunters and is frequently used for personal consumption.

Hunting water buffalo is a challenging yet rewarding endeavor that demands a strategic approach and a deep understanding of these magnificent creatures. The buffalo's strength and unpredictability demand vigilance and respect. Understanding their behavior and being prepared for sudden charges is essential for hunter safety.

SCRUB BULL
Bos taurus
Wild bull

A formidable and enigmatic game species, the scrub bull, reigns supreme. Known for its rugged and wild demeanor, the scrub bull presents a thrilling challenge for hunters venturing into the remote and unspoiled landscapes of this region. A cousin to the domesticated cattle, the scrub bull has reverted to a feral existence, embodying the spirit of the Outback and offering a true test of hunting prowess. With its massive build, keen senses, and elusive nature, pursuing the scrub bull is a quest that beckons those who seek adventure, adrenaline, and a deeper connection to the Australian wilds.

Hunters in Australia's Northern Territory often refer to the scrub bull as "scrubbies." Similar to the water buffalo the scrubbies are big, muscular creatures with strong physiques making them a challenging quarry for hunters making their hunting adventurous. Their sturdy legs and well-defined hooves enable them to traverse the rugged terrain with agility and grace. Prominent, curved horns of the males are both impressive trophies and formidable weapons, accentuating the thrill and danger of the hunt. As hunters track scrubbies through the thick brush and remote wilderness, they are captivated by the interplay of these animals' robust structure and their natural instincts, creating an exhilarating experience that embodies the essence of wild game hunting in the Australian Outback.

They can weigh anywhere from 1,100 to 1,600 pounds (500 to 725 kilograms) or more while in terms of length, a mature scrub bull can measure around 6 to 7 feet (1.8 to 2.1 meters) from its head to the base of the tail, with the tail adding an additional 2 to 3 feet (0.6 to 0.9 meters). Many hunters and culinary enthusiasts find scrub bull meat to be delicious. It is often described as lean, flavorful, and rich, with a distinct and sometimes stronger taste compared to beef from domestic cattle. These feral descendants of domestic cattle have adapted to a rugged existence in the country's northern regions. Their habitat spans across diverse terrains, from dense tropical woodlands and savannas to arid outback plains, often characterized by harsh environmental conditions. Scrub bulls graze on native grasses, shrubs, and forage for sustenance, their robust physique well-suited to the challenging terrain.

WILD BOAR
Sus scrofa

Wild boars, often dubbed "federal pigs," reign as a challenging game species for hunters. These formidable creatures have adapted to the region's diverse habitats, from lush tropical forests to arid scrublands, displaying an indomitable spirit. Wild boars, omnivorous by nature, have a voracious appetite, foraging on a diverse diet that includes roots, fruits, insects, and small mammals. Breeding during the wet season, these pigs embark on thrilling mating rituals that add to the excitement of the hunt. Their tusks, sharp and imposing, serve as both tools and weapons, and their elusive nature keeps hunters engaged and alert in the rugged terrain. With weights reaching up to 300 pounds (136 kilograms) or more, bagging a wild boar is not just a triumph of skill, but a reward of succulent and highly sought-after meat. The sheer thrill of tracking and capturing these wily creatures, combined with the culinary delight they offer, makes wild boar hunting an irresistible adventure in the Northern Territory's untamed wilds.

DONKEY
Equus africanus asinus

An unexpected and exhilarating pursuit for hunters has emerged - the donkey. Originally brought to the continent for labor, these domesticated equines have found an unlikely home in the rugged Australian outback. Donkeys have adapted to a lifestyle reminiscent of their wild ancestors by roaming freely through diverse habitats, from arid deserts to lush savannas. Their voracious appetite includes foraging on a variety of vegetation, making them a resourceful survivor in the region's challenging conditions. Breeding throughout the year, donkeys have become an enticing game for hunters, with the thrill of tracking and capturing these resilient animals adding to the excitement. Weighing up to 600 kilograms (1,300 pounds) or more, the promise of lean, succulent donkey meat provides a rewarding culinary aspect to this unique hunting endeavor, turning the quest for these domesticated equines into an adventurous and flavorful pursuit that captivates the hearts of Australian hunters.

BRUMBY
Wild horse
Equus ferus caballus

The brumby, Australia's wild horse, commands the rugged landscapes with a spirit as untamed as the land itself. Their ability to adapt to the area's harsh conditions is demonstrated by their food, consisting of local grasses and bushes. Brumbies breed all year long, making them an alluring target for hunters who enjoy the rush of following these nimble and cunning animals. Given that mature brumbies can weigh up to 1,200 pounds (545 kilograms) or more, the possibility of luscious, lean horse flesh brings a special gourmet dimension to this exciting hunting experience, fusing adventure, tradition, and a strong bond with the wild spirit of the Australian Outback.

BANTENG
Bos javanicus
Wild cattle

Particularly in comparison to the scrub bull and water
buffalo, banteng is recognized for its powerful and muscular
build as well as its stunning horns, which serve as hunting
trophies. As they can only be found in the Cobourg Peninsula,
bantengs are extremely rare, which makes hunting them both
thrilling and challenging. A mature banteng can weigh over
1,200 pounds (545 kilograms), which ensures a satisfying
harvest of flavorful, lean meat from the untamed Outback.
Banteng, on average, can typically measure around 5 to 6 feet

(1.5 to 1.8 meters) in shoulder height. Their length, from their head to the base of the tail, can range from approximately 6 to 7.5 feet (1.8 to 2.3 meters).

The wet season signals the breeding season, which heightens the hunt's thrill as hunters negotiate difficult terrain and unpredictably changing weather.

SMALL GAME AND UPLAND BIRDS

MAGPIE GOOSE
Anseranas semipalmata

The striking beauty of the magpie goose captures the hearts of hunters and nature enthusiasts alike. With its striking black and white plumage and a graceful, slender neck, the magpie goose is a mesmerizing sight against the backdrop of shimmering waterways and lush reed beds. These magnificent birds are not only a testament to nature's artistry but also a coveted game species for those who relish the thrill of waterfowl hunting. Their annual migrations signal the beginning of the waterfowl hunting season, when hunters are lured to these wetlands to partake in the beauty and difficulty of the magpie goose hunt, making it an alluring activity for anybody seeking both a beautiful marvel and the thrill of the wild.

PACIFIC BLACK DUCK
Anas superciliosa

The Pacific black duck, with its understated elegance, assumes a distinctive role in the world of waterfowl hunting. Cloaked in dark plumage and marked by a striking white eye ring, this duck's beauty is both subtle and captivating. Its graceful presence against the shimmering, mirror-like surfaces of lagoons and billabongs creates a sense of tranquility in the midst of the rugged wilderness. The Pacific black duck is an understated yet highly prized game bird, adding an element of challenge and intrigue to the art of waterfowl hunting. While their appearance may be unassuming, their elusiveness and the skill required to pursue them make hunting the Pacific black duck an engaging and rewarding pursuit, uniting the thrill of the hunt with an appreciation for the serenity of their wetland habitat.

GALAH
Eolophus roseicapilla

With its distinct attractiveness, the galah emerges as a desirable game bird for hunters. The galah stands out as a distinctive species, offering an alluring contrast against the rough Outback landscape with its decorations of delicate pink and soft gray. Both fascinating and stunning, these sociable and playful birds liven up the Northern Territory's skies with their vibrant presence. The galah's attraction as a game bird adds an exciting dimension to hunting in this area, in addition to being frequently admired for their vivid plumage and energetic calls. Hunting the galah is a captivating adventure that combines an appreciation of their distinctive beauty with the excitement of the pursuit, not simply because of their outstanding appearance but also because of the difficulty of pursuing these nimble and evasive animals.

HUNTING LOCATIONS AND OUTFITTERS

Northern Territory reveals itself as an extraordinary canvas for the fearless hunter.

From the Red Center's arid deserts to Top End's lush wetlands, this region beckons with an allure that only the wild can offer. For those seeking the ultimate hunting adventure, the Northern Territory presents many enticing locations, each with its distinct charm.

In the Top End, the thriving wetlands unfurl before the hunter's eager eyes, creating a waterfowl paradise. Famed for its magpie geese, wild ducks, and other waterfowl, these shimmering wetlands promise an exhilarating experience for waterfowl enthusiasts. The lush landscapes are transformed into a hunter's haven during the waterfowl season, attracting those who revel in the thrill of the chase amidst nature's elegance.

For those with a penchant for wild cattle, the remote outback savannas and thickets of the Northern Territory hold an irresistible appeal. Here, the elusive scrub bulls, descendants of domesticated cattle, roam freely, presenting a challenge that only these sturdy terrains can offer. With a landscape defined by eucalypt woodlands, open plains, and the ever-present red earth, the outback epitomizes the essence of Australian wilderness.

Hunters frequently rely on the seasoned expertise of outfitters who are intimately familiar with the subtleties of the game and terrain in the Northern Territory to navigate this wild paradise with finesse. These guides and local experts are of great assistance, ensuring that the hunting trip is not only successful but also morally and environmentally responsible.

GEAR AND EQUIPMENT

Gear is like alcohol. As you age, you come to understand that quality is more important than quantity. That basic statement holds true for the hunter—save your money and focus on getting yourself into a kit of quality gear rather than cutting corners by buying a bunch of subpar junk that brings you lots of frustration and not much game meat. Northern

Territory of Australia, the pursuit of game requires a comprehensive arsenal of gear and equipment to navigate the strong terrain and secure a safe and successful hunt. The linchpin of any hunter's inventory includes a suitable firearm and an ample supply of ammunition, handpicked in accordance with local laws. The essential hunting knife stands as a symbol of field expertise, indispensable for field dressing and game preparation. Optics, ranging from high-quality binoculars to precision rifle scopes, offer the advantage of spotting game from a distance and ensuring accurate shots.

The wardrobe of a seasoned hunter mirrors the conditions of the environment, consisting of camouflage attire for blending with the landscape, breathable and weather-resistant clothing suited to the season, and sturdy boots with reliable traction. A well-organized backpack serves as a mobile command center, housing essential items, such as a hydration system to counteract the Australian sun's relentless assault. A navigational toolkit, comprising GPS devices, compasses, and topographic maps, becomes the compass to navigate the bush and mark hunting sites.

Safety is still top priority, and binoculars are kept safely within reach thanks to a well-designed harness and a comprehensive first-aid kit for minor injuries and emergencies. With the aid of game calls and an ammunition belt or pouch, skilled hunters can lure their prey, and when the time is right, they can quickly reload.

Regulatory documents, such as hunting licenses and game tags, are imperative to comply with local laws and quotas, and a reliable rangefinder assists in gauging accurate shot distances.

Resting at the core of the hunter's equipment list is a durable and dependable backpack, designed to accommodate all essential gear, from optics and clothing to water and field dressing tools. A water and hydration system ensures that dehydration remains a distant concern, particularly under the unforgiving Australian sun. Provisions for insect repellent to ward off persistent insects, ample lighting with headlamps or flashlights for the low light hours, and personal safety gear, including whistles and signaling devices, are vital for security and survival in the vast, isolated landscapes. To maintain the integrity of the harvest, insulating game bags or a portable cooler must be at the ready. With the ability to process your harvest efficiently, a field dressing kit with gloves and essential tools stands as an unyielding companion. To round off the hunter's inventory, a survival kit, sunscreen, sunglasses, and a wide-brimmed hat safeguard against the harsh and sometimes unrelenting Australian elements.

TECHNIQUES AND STRATEGIES

Hunting in the Northern Territory of Australia demands a nuanced approach, as the region's diverse terrains, fluctuating climates, and abundant wildlife require a thoughtful blend of technique and strategy.

Understanding the local wildlife, their habits, and the seasonal changes is crucial first and foremost. There are numerous game species in the Northern Territory, each with distinctive behavioral traits and habitat preferences. When it comes to finding game, locating feeding and watering areas, and predicting their movements, time invested in careful research and scouting pays off.

The region's stark contrasts in vegetation and topography require hunters to adapt their camouflage tactics. Patience is a virtue in the often hot and arid conditions, with the benefit of waiting quietly for game to come to you.

Knowledge of the local environment, including topographical features, water sources, and prevailing winds, is integral to selecting strategic hunting locations. Wind direction plays a critical role in approaching game, as animals have a keen sense of smell. Identifying areas where wind conditions are favorable is a key component of successful hunting.

Collaboration with knowledgeable outfitters or regional guides also provides invaluable insight into the specifics of hunting in the Northern Territory. They have an advantage in tracking and approaching game because they are aware about the area's wildlife, terrain, and local laws.

Utilizing the appropriate gear and equipment, from firearms and optics to navigation tools, is crucial, and ensuring that all equipment is maintained and in optimal working condition is a vital element of any successful hunt.

ADVENTURE AND CULTURE

the Northern Territory is a place where the culture of hunting intertwines with Indigenous traditions. The respect for game, the land, and the wildlife is deeply ingrained in the region's hunting practices.

As hunters traverse the untamed landscapes, they have the opportunity to connect with the region's rich Indigenous culture, which has coexisted with these lands for millennia. The traditions, stories, and art of the First Nations people become an integral part of the hunting adventure, adding depth and significance to the experience.

The Northern Territory's abundant wildlife, whether it's waterfowl, wild cattle, or other game species, offers thrilling challenges and rewarding pursuits. It's a place where the thrill of the chase is amplified by the vastness of the terrain and the unique character of the game species.

In essence, the Northern Territory represents a unique and unforgettable destination for hunters, where the adventure is enhanced by a profound connection to the region's Indigenous culture and the untamed spirit of Australia's Outback.

STRAIGHT FROM THE AUTHOR A TALE TO REMEMBER

8 am, finally the day I waited for the longest: hunting in Australia! Me, along with my professional hunter Hayden, were off to our new hunting adventure. Hopefully, the best one so far!

9 am, we grabbed our wallets, fully loaded wallets, making sure to get a big healthy breakfast to prepare ourselves for the long, tiring day in Australia. 11 am, grabbed our bags, got our

rifles, a quick check to our rifles, and headed to our prolonged journey. Professional hunter Hayden and I got our rifles and headed to the airport on our way to Australia. I thought we were leaving on our flight to Australia on a plane; however, to my surprise, Hunter Hayden got us a helicopter! Already an amazing start to hopefully an amazing day! Hunting in a helicopter? For sure, a dream come true!

A long journey to Australia, but gladly, we would reach there sooner thanks to hunter Hayden and his helicopter. A lifesaver for sure! As soon as we began to reach our destination, we came across a remote location, a creek system. The lack of a road system next to the creek system, an incredibly unsettling area without a suitable place to land our helicopter, was more troubling.

We decided to ignore the area due to the rough land and nowhere to land our helicopter. That was when, around the bend, we saw a giant bull, almost 10 feet tall, standing 20 yards away, hidden under the strip of trees right on the edge of the top of the hill. We were not entirely sure if it was a bull as it hid very well under the trees. Our pilot had seen water Buffalo bulls in the last couple of weeks, so my Professional Hunter Hayden and I decided to walk down the creek beds and give our luck a shot.

We safely walked down the helicopter into the creek bed and headed to the hill, where we saw the bull. Walking on the rough wetland with rifles and our stuffed bags was painful, but hopefully, it would be worth the adventure. Just as we reached the trees, the bull ran off! Hard luck. But thank our good fortune, it was a water buffalo! It would surely be a great win and a massive reward if we got this.

We ran behind the water buffalo until it hid in the trees again. This time, without uttering a word or making any sound, we started walking towards the trees. We kept looking for any signs but unfortunately couldn't find it. Losing hope, we decided to head back, and exactly at that moment, my Professional hunter spotted him. I raised the 375 CZ Rifle and quickly shot a series of four times to put the big buffalo down. We got it! A full of thrill win, indeed. Huge 10-foot-long water buffalo with beautiful horns as a reward and a ton of juicy, tasty meat all ready to go back with us.

Finally, we took our pictures for the great win. The meat was cut, can not wait to have it. A beautiful win always tastes ten times better than any normal animal ever would. We caped the buffalo, and it was taken in the helicopter.

It was time to head back when, on our way, my outfitter shot a big pig, a great win for him, too! What a day it was, everyone. When we thought it was surely the end of the trip, we sat back on the helicopter and made our way back home. We saw donkeys while returning and gladly had a chance to snipe them from a helicopter using a 243 semi-automatic rifle with a red dot sight, and there's that: a successful kill!

What a journey! Helicopter, water buffalo, big pig, and donkeys? An incredible journey, full of thrill, adventure, and massive wins. Surely the best one yet! A great day for everyone, indeed!

Chapter 8:
Tasmania

Tasmania is known for its devils. The Tasmanian devils. They were seen as a threat to livestock in Tasmania. Devils were hunted until 1941 when they became officially protected. But sadly, as they were persecuted to near extinction, the population has struggled to recover. Since 2008, Tasmanian devils have been listed as Endangered to extinction. However, Tasmania still has great games and a beautiful view that serves as peace to the eyes in the thrilling adventure. Whether you are a deer hunter or a mad, crazy duck hunter, Tasmania is the right place for you. From beautiful fallow deer to wallabies, kangaroos, and mutton birds, Tasmania has it all. There are also several species that can be hunted under crop protection permits. Even if you are visiting from overseas or from another Australian state, Tasmania has game opportunities for everyone, offering both thrill and adventure.

Game Species in Tasmania

WALLABIES
Macropus spp.
Graceful Bounders of Tasmania

The Wallaby, belonging to the Macropus genus, graces the rough landscapes of Tasmania, Australia, adding a unique dimension to the hunting experience. Known for their graceful bounding and nimble movements, wallabies are sought after by hunters for their clever and challenging pursuits. Wallabies in Tasmania exhibit distinct characteristics that make them intriguing targets. The various species within the Macropus genus, such as the Bennett's Wallaby and the Swamp Wallaby, vary in size and coloration. Bennett's Wallabies, for instance, have a brownish-gray fur coat with a white underside, while Swamp Wallabies display a darker, more robust appearance.

Hunting wallabies in Tasmania requires careful consideration of the diverse territories and land classifications. Crown land, encompassing public land owned by the state, often provides accessible hunting opportunities. However, hunters need to get the required licenses and follow certain rules regarding the use of firearms and hunting seasons. Private landowners may grant permission for wallaby hunting, but it is essential to secure explicit consent and comply with any conditions set by the landowner. Public land, including reserves and national parks, presents additional challenges, with strict regulations in place to protect the environment and native wildlife. Hunters must follow designated trails and adhere to established guidelines to minimize impact.

State forests, characterized by expansive woodlands, are often home to wallaby populations. Accessing these areas for hunting necessitates awareness of forest regulations, permit requirements, and designated hunting zones. Conservation areas aimed at protecting biodiversity may have restricted hunting permissions or seasonal restrictions to safeguard vulnerable species. Wallaby hunters in Tasmania should be familiar with the specific regulations governing each type of land, respecting both legal obligations and environmental conservation efforts.

Tasmania is renowned for its wallaby hunting opportunities, drawing enthusiasts from far and wide. The challenging landscape, diverse wallaby species, and severe regulations contribute to the allure of the pursuit. Wallaby hunting demands a combination of stealth, marksmanship, and knowledge of the terrain. The animals' keen senses and rapid movements require hunters to adapt to the dynamic nature of the chase. The thrill of tracking wallabies through Tasmania's breathtaking landscapes adds an element of adventure and excitement to the experience.

KANGAROO
Macropodidae
The Red Giants of The Forest

The forest kangaroo, a majestic member of the Macropodidae family, adds a distinct appeal to hunting expeditions in Tasmania, especially in the Midland and North East corners of the island. With its imposing stature and reddish-brown fur, the forest kangaroo, often identified as the Tasmanian Forester Kangaroo (Macropus giganteus tasmaniensis), stands out as a challenging and captivating quarry for hunters. These red giants roam the dense woodlands and thrive in the unique ecosystems of Tasmania, contributing to the rich biodiversity of the region.

Understanding the legal aspects of kangaroo hunting is paramount for hunters in Tasmania. While hunting kangaroos is legal, strict regulations are in place to manage populations and ensure sustainable practices. Hunters must obtain the appropriate permits and observe hunting seasons, bag limits, and other guidelines set by wildlife authorities. Responsible hunting is crucial to maintaining the ecological balance and conserving these iconic marsupials.

In the Midland and North East corners of Tasmania, where the forest kangaroo thrives, hunters encounter a land that demands both skill and resilience. Navigating through the dense forests and undulating landscapes requires a keen understanding of the kangaroo's behavior and preferred habitats. The thrill of tracking these elusive creatures amidst the towering trees and lush vegetation adds an extra layer of excitement to the hunting experience.

Engaging in forest kangaroo hunting in Tasmania provides a unique opportunity for hunters to connect with the rich cultural and natural tapestry of the region. The pursuit of these red giants is not merely a recreational activity but a chance to immerse oneself in the history and traditions woven into the land. As hunters venture into the Midland and North East corners, they become part of a narrative that spans generations, where the forest kangaroo serves as a symbol of resilience, survival, and the intricate relationship between humans and the wild.

FALLOW DEER
Dama dama
Ghost of the forest

Tasmania has a fantastic deer hunting season running through a ballot system opening in December and ending in January each year. Tasmania is famous for its exclusive fallow deer hunting as they are the only deer species found in Tasmania.

Their antlers are what attracts the hunters to Tasmania. Although you require a game license for hunting fallow deer, it's worth the price.

SMALL GAME AND UPLAND BIRDS

MUTTON BIRD
Puffinus tenuirostris
A thrilling pursuit

There is a strong tradition around mutton birding in Tasmania that has been practiced both by settlers and Indigenous tribes of Tasmania. Muttonbirding is the term used to describe the seasonal harvesting of mutton bird (or short-tailed shearwater) chicks. To legally hunt mutton birds in Tasmania, you must hold a valid game license (which costs $32.40). There are also strict daily bag limits, a limited number of colonies that can be hunted, and a short window in which you can legally hunt mutton birds.

Tasmania proudly boasts the claim as the exclusive habitat for these fascinating birds, making Mutton Bird hunting a distinctive and thrilling effort for enthusiastic hunters.

Mutton Birds are migratory seabirds that travel thousands of kilometers to breed exclusively in Tasmania during the southern hemisphere's spring and summer. Their arrival heralds the beginning of the hunting season, drawing enthusiasts from around the world.

Thrill-seeking hunters, fascinated by the challenge of catching these swift and agile birds, eagerly await the hunting season. The Mutton Bird's night habits add an extra layer of excitement to the hunt as hunters navigate the rugged coastal landscapes under the veil of darkness. Armed with specialized tools like long-handled nets, hunters venture to the nesting grounds, often located on remote and wind-swept islands along Tasmania's coastline.

Mutton Bird hunting is not just about the thrill of the chase; it carries deep cultural significance in Tasmania. Local communities have engaged in this practice for generations, passing down traditional knowledge and techniques. The process involves carefully extracting the fledgling Mutton Birds, known as 'muttons,' from their burrows, and their oil-rich flesh is considered a delicacy. The experience is a unique blend of adventure, cultural immersion, and culinary delight.

Participating in Mutton Bird hunting requires adherence to strict regulations, including licensing and quotas, to ensure sustainable practices. Conservation efforts play a crucial role in preserving the delicate balance of the Mutton Bird population, and hunters contribute to the ongoing research and protection of these remarkable seabirds.

GREY TEAL
Anas gracilis
A Waterfowl Adventure

Hunters eagerly anticipate the arrival of the Grey Teal (Anas gracilis), marking the beginning of an exhilarating waterfowl hunting season. These sleek and agile ducks, distinguished by their mottled grey plumage and distinctive teal-colored wing patches, are a prized target for waterfowl enthusiasts seeking both challenge and connection to Tasmania's rich natural heritage.

The Grey Teal, with its adaptability to diverse habitats, is a migratory species that frequents Tasmania's wetlands and estuaries. What sets Grey Teal hunting apart is the dynamic nature of pursuing these waterfowl in their varied environments. Hunters must navigate through reed-filled marshes, navigate riverbanks, and set up blinds strategically to outwit the keen senses of the Grey Teal.

Waterfowl hunters, drawn to the thrill of the chase and the challenge of mimicking the calls and behaviors of their elusive prey, find Grey Teal hunting to be an immersive and rewarding experience. The ducks' acrobatic flight patterns and cautious nature require a combination of skill, patience, and strategic planning, adding an element of excitement to the pursuit.

Tasmania's wetlands and estuaries provide an ideal backdrop for Grey Teal hunting, attracting hunters from far and wide. The seasonal nature of waterfowl hunting, coupled with the need for specific gear such as decoys, calls, and appropriate firearms, contributes to the camaraderie and shared passion among waterfowl enthusiasts.

MALLARD DUCK
Anas platyrhynchos
Pursuing the Vibrant Aviator

The Mallard Duck (Anas platyrhynchos), with its vibrant plumage and distinctive quacking calls, adds a dynamic dimension to waterfowl hunting in Tasmania. While Mallard Ducks are not native to the island, they have established thriving populations, attracting hunters with their lively presence in Tasmania's wetlands, rivers, and lakes.

Mallard Ducks are legally hunted in Tasmania, but hunters must obey to specific regulations to ensure sustainable practices and conservation efforts. Bag limits, hunting seasons, and designated areas are in place to manage the Mallard Duck population and protect the broader ecosystem. Responsible hunters obtain the necessary permits, stay informed about regulations, and contribute to the preservation of Tasmania's diverse waterfowl habitats.

Mallard Ducks exhibit sexual dimorphism, with males (drakes) showcasing vibrant iridescent plumage, while females (hens) have more camouflaged colors for nesting. Mallards are versatile in their habitats, thriving in both natural and human-altered environments. Their adaptability to diverse wetland ecosystems makes them an enticing target for waterfowl hunters seeking varied and challenging environments.

BLUE-BILLED DUCK
Oxyura australis
The Quest for Avian Elegance

The Blue-billed Duck (Oxyura australis), an avian spectacle with its striking cobalt-blue bill and intricate plumage, elevates waterfowl hunting in Tasmania to an artful pursuit. Although not native to the island, these ducks have found a

151

niche in Tasmania's wetlands, offering hunters a captivating and unique target.

Hunting the Blue-billed Duck in Tasmania requires adherence to legal guidelines and conservation efforts. While they are not as commonly hunted as some other waterfowl species, responsible hunters obtain the necessary permits, stay informed about regulations, and contribute to the preservation of Tasmania's diverse waterfowl habitats. Bag limits and designated hunting seasons are in place to ensure sustainable practices, fostering a balance between recreational hunting and conservation.

Engaging in Blue-billed Duck hunting requires specialized gear, including decoys, calls, and shotguns with appropriate ammunition. The ducks' cautious nature and rapid flight patterns demand a strategic approach from hunters. Navigating Tasmania's wetlands, hunters often find themselves in well-concealed blinds or utilizing watercraft to approach their elusive quarry stealthily.

Tasmania's wetlands provide a picturesque setting for Blue-billed Duck hunting, where the convergence of avian elegance and hunter skill creates a unique experience. Beyond the thrill of the chase, waterfowl hunters in Tasmania actively contribute to the broader conservation efforts, recognizing the importance of preserving the delicate balance of the island's ecosystems.

Blue-billed Duck hunting in Tasmania offers waterfowl enthusiasts a distinctive and visually enchanting pursuit. The legal considerations, combined with the elegance of the ducks and the strategic elements of the hunt, make this endeavor both challenging and rewarding. Engaging in Blue-billed Duck hunting in Tasmania becomes not just a recreational activity but a celebration of the intricate beauty and diversity of the island's waterfowl habitats.

HUNTING LOCATIONS AND OUTFITTERS

Tasmania, Australia, stands as a premier destination for hunting enthusiasts, offering diverse landscapes and a wealth of game species. The island's vast wilderness encompasses a range of terrains, from dense forests and wetlands to open plains, providing a variety of hunting experiences. For those seeking professional guidance and support, numerous outfitters in Tasmania cater to the needs of both novice and seasoned hunters. These outfitters typically offer guided hunting expeditions, ensuring participants navigate the challenging landscapes with safety and expertise. Experienced guides are well-versed in the behaviors of the local wildlife, providing valuable insights for a successful hunt. The selection of hunting locations varies, with options such as Crown land, private estates, state forests, and designated conservation areas. Each location presents unique challenges and opportunities, contributing to the diversity of the hunting experience. Private landowners often collaborate with outfitters to provide exclusive access to prime hunting grounds, while public lands and state forests offer expansive territories for those seeking a more adventurous and independent hunt. When selecting an outfitter in Tasmania, it's crucial to consider their reputation, knowledge of local regulations, and commitment to ethical and sustainable hunting practices. Many outfitters also assist with logistics, including permits, accommodations, and transportation, ensuring hunters can focus on the thrill of the chase. With its rich biodiversity and well-managed hunting opportunities, Tasmania remains a sought-after destination for those looking to embark on memorable and rewarding hunting adventures.

GEAR AND EQUIPMENT

The island's diverse topography, including dense rainforests, rugged mountains, and coastal plains, demands specialized gear for an enriching experience. Selecting the right firearm is crucial, with bolt-action rifles in calibers such as .270 Winchester or .308 Winchester proving versatile for the diverse game species like red deer and wallabies that inhabit Tasmania. Adherence to stringent firearms regulations is paramount, ensuring a responsible approach to the pursuit.

If you are visiting Tasmania from another Australian state or territory, you do not need to apply for an exemption and can legally hunt in Tasmania as long as you hold a corresponding license issued in your home state or territory. You will, however, need to apply for a Tasmanian game license, where applicable, for the species you wish to hunt.

Navigating Tasmania's dense wilderness requires robust optics, emphasizing the need for high-quality binoculars and a reliable rifle scope. The island's temperamental weather necessitates adaptable clothing, with waterproof and breathable layers essential for the often unpredictable conditions. Camouflaged or earth-toned attire becomes not just a choice but a strategic necessity in the intricate and varied landscapes where stealth is paramount. Sturdy and comfortable footwear, including waterproof boots, is indispensable for traversing diverse territories, from muddy rainforests to rocky alpine slopes.

A spacious and durable backpack proves essential for carrying provisions, first aid supplies, and additional clothing layers, catering to Tasmania's ever-changing weather patterns.

Given the island's pristine environment, responsible hunters equip themselves with navigation tools like GPS devices or topographic maps to ensure a respectful and minimal impact on the ecosystem. Tasmania's diverse game, including the elusive Tasmanian deer and native waterfowl, necessitates the inclusion of a reliable hunting knife for field dressing and processing game.

Moreover, engaging with knowledgeable local outfitters is integral to a successful Tasmanian hunting experience. These seasoned guides offer insights into the nuances of Tasmania's unique landscapes, from the rugged Southwest National Park to the coastal wetlands, enhancing the hunter's understanding of the region. Tasmania, with its distinct blend of natural beauty and challenging terrains, beckons hunters to embrace the adventure with a set of gear tailored to navigate its intricacies responsibly and skillfully.

TECHNIQUES AND STRATEGIES

Hunting in Tasmania, Australia, demands a nicety approach, blending diverse techniques and strategic insights to navigate the island's unique challenges and capitalize on its rich biodiversity. Tasmania's game, including Tasmanian deer and wallabies, requires a thorough understanding of their behavior and habitat. Stalking proves to be an effective technique, particularly in the dense rainforests and rugged mountains where game may be elusive. Mastering the art of stealth and patience is crucial as hunters navigate through the intricate landscapes, relying on keen observational skills to spot and approach their quarry.

In Tasmania's expansive wilderness, spot-and-stalk hunting becomes a valuable strategy, especially in the open alpine areas where visibility is greater. Elevated positions provide vantage points for hunters to survey the terrain and identify the game from a distance. Additionally, waterfowl enthusiasts exploring the coastal wetlands should employ effective calling techniques to attract the diverse birdlife that frequents the island's waterways.

Understanding the seasonal patterns and migrations of the game is vital for successful hunting in Tasmania. Different regions and elevations may present varying opportunities throughout the year, necessitating a flexible approach to hunting locations and timing. Local knowledge, whether gained through experience or consultation with seasoned guides, becomes invaluable for hunters seeking to unravel the nuances of Tasmania's dynamic ecosystems.

Navigating Tasmania's challenging terrain demands proficient tracking skills, as game may leave subtle signs in the form of tracks, droppings, and disturbed vegetation. Hunters should equip themselves with reliable navigation tools, such as GPS devices or topographic maps, to explore the diverse landscapes responsibly and avoid getting disoriented.

Collaboration with experienced local outfitters is paramount. These guides, well-versed in Tasmania's unique landscapes, contribute valuable insights into regional hunting strategies, wildlife behaviors, and the best practices for ethical and responsible hunting. By combining these techniques and strategies, hunters can optimize their chances of a successful and rewarding hunting experience in Tasmania's captivating and varied outdoors.

ADVENTURE AND CULTURE

Tasmania, Australia, unfolds as an enthralling canvas for hunters, presenting a distinct adventure and culture that sets it apart in the world of hunting. The island's unique charm lies in its diverse landscapes, ranging from dense rainforests to rugged mountains and coastal plains. Tasmania's hunting culture is characterized by a deep connection to the pristine environment, where hunters embrace a harmonious relationship with the natural world. The pursuit of game, including Tasmanian deer and wallabies, is not just a sport but a journey into the heart of the island's untamed wilderness.

The adventure in Tasmania is marked by the challenge of navigating intricate lands, from the lush expanses of Cradle Mountain to the hidden valleys of Southwest National Park. Unlike anywhere else, Tasmania's game requires hunters to be adept at both stalking through dense vegetation and spotting game in the open alpine regions. The experience is a delicate dance with nature, where every step unveils the island's rich biodiversity and demands a keen understanding of the unique behaviors of Tasmanian wildlife.

The cultural aspect of hunting in Tasmania reflects a deep respect for the island's indigenous heritage and the diverse ecosystems that sustain its game. Hunters often engage with local communities, learning from their wisdom about the land and its creatures. Tasmania's hunting culture thrives on storytelling, where tales of successful pursuits and encounters with the island's iconic wildlife are shared around campfires, creating a sense of camaraderie among hunters.

Moreover, Tasmania's emphasis on ethical and sustainable hunting practices adds a layer of responsibility to the cultural narrative. Hunters in Tasmania actively participate in conservation efforts, contributing to the preservation of the